SIXTH GRADE MATH
Table of Contents

SIXTH GRADE MATH

Introduction

Mathematics skills are utilized in every aspect of an individual's life, whether a student or an adult. These skills, however, involve more than just the computation of numbers. Organization, investigation, logical reasoning, and communication are also basic skills associated with mathematics. Students must develop a solid foundation in basic mathematics skills in order to meet the challenges of learning. Once armed with these tools, they can face new situations with confidence in their ability to solve problems and to make decisions.

The *Sixth Grade Math* program is offered to develop and strengthen mathematics skills. Each page provides practice in one specified skill. The worksheet can be used to assess students' understanding of the concept before or after the classroom lesson, or it can be used by students who might benefit from additional practice, either at home or school.

Organization

Nine units cover the basic mathematics skills taught in the sixth grade. Students begin with a review of place value and adding and subtracting whole numbers and decimals. They move on to practice skills dealing with multiplication and division of whole numbers and decimals. Students then proceed to explore essential skills involving fractions and measurement. Finally, the book focuses on geometry, graphs, and ratios, proportions, and percents. Fun, thematic worksheet titles attract students' interest. One page at the end of each unit is devoted solely to word problems which show how the learned skill might be applied to real-world situations. These problems also provide practice in using a variety of problem-solving strategies.

Special Features

Each worksheet serves as practice for only one basic mathematics skill. Students who may need additional practice could benefit from these pages. Each page in the *Sixth Grade Math* book also ends with a word problem. These problems deal only with the skill students are practicing. These word problems also provide examples of how mathematics skills can be applied to the real world.

Use

This book is designed for independent use by students who have had instruction in the specific skills covered in the lessons. Copies of the worksheets can be given to individuals, pairs of students, or small groups for completion. The worksheets can also be given as homework for reviewing and reinforcing basic mathematics skills.

To begin, determine the implementation that fits your students' needs and your classroom structure. The following plan suggests a format for use:

1. Explain the purpose of the worksheets to your class.
2. Review the mechanics of how you want students to work with the exercises.
3. Review the specific skill for the students who may not remember the process for successful completion of the computation.
4. Introduce students to the process and to the purpose of the activities.
5. Do a practice activity together.
6. Discuss how students can use the skill as they work and play.

Additional Notes

1. A letter to parents is included on page 4. Send it home with the students and encourage them to share it with their parents.
2. Have fun with the pages. Math should be an enjoyable adventure that helps students grow, not only in math, but in their confidence and their ability to face new and challenging experiences.

Dear Parent,

Mathematics skills are important tools that your child will use throughout his or her life. These skills encompass more than just the computation of numbers. They involve the ability of individuals to organize, investigate, reason, and communicate. Thus, your child must develop a strong foundation of basic mathematics skills in the elementary grades so that he or she can expand and build on these skills to help navigate through the life experiences.

During the year, your child will be learning and practicing many mathematics skills in class. Some of the skills include computing fractions and decimals, working with graphs, and determining ratios, proportions, and percents. After exploring the concepts associated with these basic skills, your child will bring home worksheets, whether completed in class or to be completed at home, designed to further practice these skills. To help your child progress at a faster rate, please consider the following suggestions:

- Together, review the work your child brings home or completes at home. Discuss any errors, and encourage your child to correct them.
- Encourage your child to make up word problems that apply to newly learned skills.
- Guide your child to see why it is important to learn math by pointing out ways that math is used in everyday life.
- Play games and solve puzzles with your child that utilize math skills.

Thank you for your help. Your child and I appreciate your assistance and reinforcement in this learning process.

Cordially,

Name _____ Date _____

••• SUITED FOR NUMEROUS ADVENTURES •••

 Solve. Round money amounts to the nearest cent.

1. 14,098
   $- 10,123$

2. 9,198
   $+ 2,547$

3. 1,344
   $\times \quad 803$

4. $81\overline{)649}$

5. $674.65
   $\times \quad 9.4$

6. 8
   $- 3\frac{7}{10}$

7. 45.12
   $- 8.25$

8. $3\frac{9}{10}$
   $+ 3\frac{1}{2}$

9. $14\frac{7}{9}$
   $- 8\frac{8}{9}$

10. $68\overline{)\$242.76}$

11. $3.6\overline{)23.958}$

12. 0.072
   $\times \quad 6$

13. 5.95
   $\times \quad 12$

14. $8\frac{4}{5}$
   $+ 2\frac{1}{10}$

15. 5.098
   $+ 1.776$

16. 494,880
   $+ 18,423$

17. $15\frac{2}{9}$
   $- 5\frac{1}{3}$

18. $18\frac{5}{6}$
   $+ 2\frac{2}{3}$

19. $15.13 - 5.2$ _____

20. $\frac{7}{8} \div \frac{2}{5}$ _____

21. $7\frac{1}{2} + 2\frac{4}{7}$ _____

22. $1\frac{5}{6} \times 3\frac{1}{11}$ _____

23. $\frac{4}{7} \times \frac{2}{8}$ _____

24. $2\frac{1}{7} \div 3\frac{3}{4}$ _____

25. $6 \div \frac{12}{13}$ _____

26. $0.38 + 1.2$ _____

Assessment: Algorithms

Math 6, SV 8099-5

Name _____   Date _____

DAILY PROBLEMS TO SOLVE

Choose the strategy and solve.

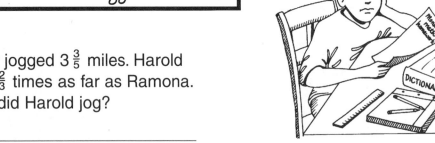

1. Ramona jogged $3\frac{3}{5}$ miles. Harold jogged $1\frac{2}{3}$ times as far as Ramona. How far did Harold jog?

_____

2. Mr. Alton is decorating tables for a party. If each table is 96 in. long, how many yards of paper will it take to cover 4 tables?

_____

3. Carla's biscuit recipe calls for $2\frac{2}{3}$ cups of flour. She wants to make $1\frac{1}{2}$ times the usual recipe. How many cups of flour will she use?

_____

4. Emily needs $3\frac{3}{4}$ yards of material to make a dress. About how many dresses can she make from 23 yards of material?

_____

5. The ratio of adults to children at a basketball game is 2 to 5. If there are 30 adults at the game, how many children are there?

_____

6. Jerry has a picture in the shape of a circle. The diameter is 46 cm. What is the circumference of the picture?

_____

7. Devon can buy 6 skeins of yarn for $8.10. If she needs 15 skeins for a project, how much will she spend on yarn?

_____

8. Ted wants to buy a camera and accessories. Of the money he has set aside, he will spend 65% on the camera, 25% on the flash, 5% on the case, and 5% on the film. Make a circle graph showing how Ted will spend his money.

_____

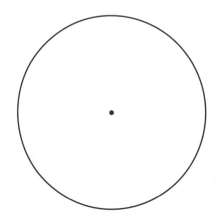

Assessment: Word Problems

Math 6, SV 8099-5

 **CAMPING OUT**

 Write the value of the underlined digit.

1. 1,3̲79,410 _____

2. 40,76̲8,319 _____

3. 64̲4,857,123 _____

Write the number in short word form.

4. 474,136 _____

5. 12,756,827 _____

6. 24,817,526,000 _____

 Write the number in standard form.

7. ten billion, eight hundred _____

8. ninety-six million, fourteen thousand, forty-eight _____

9. 4,000,000,000 + 200,000 + 90,000 + 700 + 10 + 9 _____

10. 10,000,000 + 100,000 + 60,000 + 6,000 + 20 _____

Real World Connection

Solve.

11. A recent sales report for Ike's Camping Equipment chain showed last year's sales at about $69,962,050. Write the number in short word form.

_____

Number Sense: Place Value to Billions

Name _____ Date _____

• • • • • • • • • • LESS THAN A SECOND • • • • • • • • • •

Write the number in standard decimal form.

1. fifteen and four tenths _____

2. three thousandths _____

3. eighteen ten-thousandths _____

4. one hundred fifty-nine and twelve hundredths _____

Complete the table.

	Standard Form	Short Word Form	Word Form
5.	0.2	_____	_____
6.	_____	_____	one and twenty-four hundredths
7.	_____	4 ten-thousandths	_____
8.	_____	_____	twenty-two and seventeen thousandths
9.	18.27	_____	_____ _____

Real World Connection

Solve.

10. Sam ran the 400-meter relay in 39.08 seconds. Write the time in short word form.

_____

Number Sense: Place Value to Ten Thousandths

Math 6, SV 8099-5

•••••••••• AN AVERAGE ORDER ••••••••••

Compare the numbers. Write <, >, or = .

1. 0.62 ◯ 56   **2.** 3,198 ◯ 3.918

3. 2.6000 ◯ 2.6   **4.** 651,280 ◯ 615,280

5. 86.40 ◯ 86.34   **6.** 4.340 ◯ 4.034

7. 655.155 ◯ 655.515 **8.** 43.96 ◯ 44.0

9. 32.8401 ◯ 328,401 **10.** 4.003 ◯ 4.0008

List the numbers in order from greatest to least. Use > .

11. 4,687; 4,874; 4,784 _____

12. 8.023; 8.09; 8.057 _____

13. 15.820; 15.280; 15.000 _____

14. 40,628; 34,628; 43,628 _____

15. 395.005; 395.050; 395.009 _____

Real World Connection

Solve.

16. The batting averages of four players are 0.268, 0.280, 0.299, and 0.265. Write these averages in order from greatest to least. Use > .

_____

Number Sense: Comparing and Ordering Numbers

Name _____ Date _____

• • • • • • • • • • • • • *ORBITING AROUND* • • • • • • • • • • • •

 | Estimate by rounding to the place indicated. |

1. 87

   tens _____

2. 2,741

   hundreds _____

3. $3.45

   dollar _____

4. $9.55

   10 cents _____

5. $103.48

   10 cents _____

6. 721,843

   ten thousands _____

| The number has been rounded to the place indicated. Write the least and greatest whole numbers that round to the given number. |

7. 65,000

   thousand _____

8. 30,000

   ten thousand _____

9. 800,000

   hundred thousand _____

10. 46,000,000

    million _____

Real World Connection

Solve.

11. The distance between Saturn and one of the satellites, Dione, is 377,538 km. Round this distance to the nearest ten thousand.

    _____

Name _____ Date _____

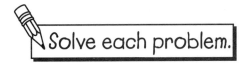

···PROBLEM SOLVING WITH POPULATIONS···

Solve each problem.

1. Manhattan Island has an area of about 89 billion, 134 million, 602 thousand, 640 square inches. Write the number in standard form.

_____

2. The subway system in New York City is two hundred thirty-one and seventy-three hundredths miles long. Write the number in standard form.

_____

3. Make a table to organize these figures from an old census. The population of each region is given below. List in order from greatest to least.

New England — 6,552,681
Middle Atlantic — 19,315,892
North Central — 18,650,621
South Atlantic — 22,432,816
East South Central — 8,489,901
West South Central — 8,534,534
Mountain — 2,633,517
Pacific — 4,192,304

4. Use your table for Exercise 4.

Was the number of people in the Middle Atlantic region closer to 19,000,000 or 20,000,000?

_____

Name _____   Date _____

•••••• "SUM" DIFFERENCES IN STORE ••••••

> Find the sum or difference. Use mental math when possible.

1. 18 + (2 + 10) = _____   **2.** 5 + 23 + 75 = _____

3. 72 + (8 + 16) = _____   **4.** (13 + 33) + 7 = _____

5. 82 + 46 + 8 = _____   **6.** 39 – 11 = _____

7. 55 + 38 + 45 = _____   **8.** 63 – 34 = _____

9. 54 + (16 + 9) = _____   **10.** 92 – 37 = _____   **11.** 12 + 23 + 38 = _____

12. 33 + (8 + 27) = _____   **13.** 16 + 25 + 24 = _____   **14.** 67 – 19 = _____

15. (14 + 78) + 66 = _____   **16.** 76 + 58 = _____   **17.** 11 + 42 + 39 = _____

18. 89 – 18 = _____   **19.** 46 + 19 + 24 = _____   **20.** 45 + 78 = _____

Real World Connection

Write the number sentence and solve.

21. Joni sold 14 sweaters, 8 pairs of jeans, and 12 shirts. How many items did she sell in all?

_____

Math 6, SV 8099-5

•••••••••••• IT'S ABOUT STAMPS ••••••••••••

 Tell whether the estimate is an overestimate or an underestimate.

1. 4,906 + 7,342 ≈ 13,000

_____

2. 78,087 + 44,329 ≈ 100,000

_____

 Use adjusted front-end estimation to estimate the sum or difference.

3. 6,219 + 4,520	**4.** 4,493 − 2,387	**5.** 3,611 + 1,922	**6.** 5,376 − 3,229

Round to estimate the sum or difference.

7. 4,320 + 3,213	**8.** 3,091 − 1,342	**9.** 9,108 + 2,547	**10.** 7,187 − 5,526
11. 49,624 + 82,107	**12.** 87,856 − 15,055	**13.** 25,197 + 34,100	**14.** 32,097 − 16,654

Real World Connection

Write the number sentence and solve.

15. Brian collected 287 foreign stamps and 625 domestic stamps during one year. About how many stamps did he collect together?

_____

Addition and Subtraction of Whole Numbers and Decimals: Estimating Whole Numbers

Math 6, SV 8099-5

•••••••••• CHECKING THE MILES ••••••••••

Find the sum or difference. Use the inverse operation to check your answer.

1. 832 _____
    + 254 _____

2. 638 _____
    − 199 _____

3. 7,323 _____
    + 2,107 _____

4. 8,145 _____
    + 7,008 _____

5. 14,098 _____
    −10,123 _____

6. 25,187 _____
    − 8,865 _____

7. 241,650 _____
    + 189,000 _____

8. 6,000,000 _____
    − 208,734 _____

Real World Connection

Solve.

9. Milagro drove 139 miles on Saturday and 185 miles on Sunday. He says he drove 324 miles altogether. Is he correct? Explain.

_____

Addition and Subtraction of Whole Numbers and Decimals: Inverse Operation

···· GETTING "CLOTHES" TO THE ANSWER ····

Use adjusted front-end estimation to estimate the sum or difference.

1. 3.6
    + 8.92

2. 2.89
    − 0.67

3. 0.67
    − 0.425

4. 0.7862
    + 0.0971

Round to estimate the sum or difference.

5. 5.98
    + 4.6

6. 13.6
    − 8.2

7. 18.4
    + 20.8

8. 3.6
    − 0.833

Estimate to compare the sum or difference. Use < or > .

9. 10.4 + 1.45 12   **10.** 24.87 − 24.02 1   **11.** 0.88 + 0.32 ◯ 0.5

Tell whether the estimate is an overestimate or an underestimate.

12. 8.6 + 9.2 ≈ 20   **13.** 6.98 + 2.43 ≈ 5   **14.** 10.4 + 8.8 ≈ 25

_____   _____   _____

Real World Connection

Write the number sentence and solve.

15. About how much will Andrea spend if she buys a skirt for $28.99, a pair of shoes for $36.25, and a blouse for $22.50?

_____

Addition and Subtraction of Whole Numbers and Decimals: Estimating Decimals

Math 6, SV 8099-5

•••••• IT'S "SNOW" PROBLEM TO ADD ••••••

Place the decimal point in the sum.

1. 6.3 + 0.26 + 14.816 = 2 1 3 7 6

2. 7.069 + 4.274 + 13.5 = 2 4 8 4 3

3. 32.09 + 8.027 + 16.8 = 5 6 9 1 7

4. 0.2 + 324.529 + 26.93 = 3 5 1 6 5 9

Find the sum.

5. 4.3 + 1.5 = _____   **6.** 23.82 + 18.8 = _____

7. $54.20 + $5.93 = _____   **8.** 65.03 + 7.468 = _____

9.   2.781   **10.**   43.17   **11.**   7.521   **12.**   4.7
     13.284   2.899   40.28   21.58
  + 6.63   + 17.4   + 0.1684   + 4.123

13. $0.45 + $62.90 + $23 = _____   **14.** 50.1 + 652.12 + 3,067 + 0.88 = _____

Real World Connection

Write the number sentence and solve.

15. The monthly snowfall during the winter was 10.5 inches, 15.85 inches, and 8.6 inches. How much snow fell?

_____

 Math 6, SV 8099-5

·········· A-DRESS THE DIFFERENCE ·········

| Place the decimal point in the difference.

1. 7.46 − 2.84 = 4 6 2

2. 17.17 − 5.7 = 1 1 4 7

3. 29.009 − 0.25 = 2 8 7 5 9

| Find the difference.

4. 9.8 − 3.95 = _____

5. 39.32 − 12.6 = _____

6. 96.111 − 7.02 = _____

7. 1.009 − 0.83 = _____

8. 7.27 − 3.621 = _____

9. 15.13 − 5.2 = _____

10. 26 − 12.274 = _____

11. 6.036 − 4.71 = _____

12. 89.5 − 30.48 = _____

13. 98 − 6.432 = _____

14. 20.22
     − 2.555

15.   4.3
     − 0.99

16. 83.8
     − 0.765

17. 78.36
     − 9.05

18. 578.32
     − 17.69

19. 57.03
     − .0041

20. 239.8
     − 73.91

21. 100.8
     − 92.44

Real World Connection

Write the number sentence and solve.

22. Luisa has 5 yards of ribbon. She uses 2.25 yards
on a dress and 1.6 yards on a blouse. How much
ribbon does she have left?

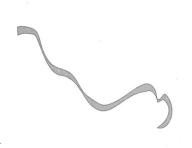

_____

Addition and Subtraction of Whole Numbers and Decimals: Subtracting Decimals

Name _____   Date _____

| Find the sum or difference. |

1. 243
    + 145

2. 5.9
    − 3.4

3. 520
    − 37

4. $12.43
    − 7.61

5. 94,880
    + 18,423

6. 4,394
    − 2,790

7. 239.8
    − 73.91

8. 465.7
    + 246.315

9. $25.53
    − 4.88

10. 23,175
    + 1,998

11. 327.51
    + 64.5

12. 4,862
    − 36.5

13. 3,091,342
    − 960,578

14. 14.9
    621.8
    + 26.93

15. 9.606 + 0.42 = _____

16. 8.43 + 1.43 = _____

17. 7.1 − 5.73 = _____

18. 13.076 + 0.08 = _____

19. 7,187 + 5,526 = _____

20. 562,391 + 39,467 = _____

Real World Connection

Write the number sentence and solve.

21. In 1900, 4,192 cars were sold. In 1910, 181,000 cars were sold. How many more were sold in 1910 than 1900?

_____

Addition and Subtraction of Whole Numbers and Decimals: Mixed Practice

                                     Math 6, SV 8099-5

Name _____ Date _____

········ MUSICAL PROBLEM SOLVING ········

Solve.

1. Lottie bought a CD of her favorite group. She paid $9.25. She bought another for $6.95. How much did Lottie spend altogether?

_____

2. Steve paid $26.25 for a 3-record album. Carlos paid $24.99 for the same album at a different store. Carlos estimated he saved $2. Steve said Carlos saved only about $1. Whose estimate is closer?

_____

3. Side A of Pedro's new tape played for 60 min. Side B played for 18.5 min. How much longer did Side A play?

_____

4. In 1997 a musician earned $2,173,556. In 1998, she earned $3,064,211. How much money did the musician earn for both years?

_____

5. Chen owns a record shop. Last year he sold $97,215 worth of merchandise. His costs were $73,110. How much profit did he make?

_____

Addition and Subtraction of Whole Numbers and Decimals: Word Problems

Name _____   Date _____

• • • • • • • • • • • • • • • BOOK MATH • • • • • • • • • • • • • • •

| Use mental math to choose the best estimate. Circle **a**, **b**, or **c**. |

1. 567×234 **a.** 100,000   **b.** 120,000   **c.** 180,000

2. 437×67 **a.** 28,000   **b.** 24,000   **c.** 35,000

3. $1,890 \times 9$ **a.** 9,000   **b.** 18,000   **c.** 21,000

4. $7,988 \times 431$ **a.** 4,000,000   **b.** 2,800,000   **c.** 3,200,000

5. $2,250 \times 52$ **a.** 100,000   **b.** 150,000   **c.** 180,000

| Estimate the product. |

6. 67
    $\times\ 7$

7. 7,912
    $\times\ \ \ 6$

8. 88
    $\times\ 4$

9. 725
    $\times\ \ 3$

10. 236
    $\times\ \ 9$

11. 519
    $\times\ \ 3$

12. 121
    $\times\ \ 4$

13. 2,017
    $\times\ \ \ \ 8$

| Estimate to compare. Use $<$ or $>$. |

14. 35×45 ◯ 2,500   **15.** 56×23 ◯ 1,000   **16.** 8×46 ◯ 600

17. 175×27 ◯ 4,000   **18.** 60×49 ◯ 2,000   **19.** 367×42 ◯ 18,000

Real World Connection

Write the number sentence and solve.

20. Each bookcase in Carla's bookstore holds 219 books. About how many books do 38 bookcases hold?

Mystery!

_____

Multiplication of Whole Numbers and Decimals: Estimating Products

Math 6, SV 8099-5

········ PRODUCTS FROM ORANGES ········

Find the product.

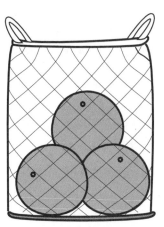

1. 68
     × 76

2. 74
     × 93

3. 2,987
     × 33

4. 1,344
     × 803

5. 46,099
     ×   35

6. 235
     × 476

7. 2,356
     × 758

8. 156,472
     ×   56

9. 10,200
     ×   503

10. 12,030
      ×   607

11. 536
      × 478

12. 5,721
      × 587

13. 7,124
      ×   63

14. 56,812
      ×   467

15. $93 \times 46 =$ _____

16. $612 \times 24 =$ _____

17. $15 \times 301 =$ _____

18. $7,503 \times 304 =$ _____

Real World Connection

Write the number sentence and solve.

19. There are 264 oranges in a large crate. How many
oranges are in 25 crates?

_____

Name _____ Date _____

•••••••••••• BUILDING PRODUCTS ••••••••••••

Choose the correct product. Circle **a**, **b**, or **c**.

1. 167×3.78

    a. 631.26

    b. 63.126

    c. 6.3126

2. 8.342×576

    a. 480,499.2

    b. 48,049.92

    c. 4,804.992

3. 56.9×25

    a. 142.25

    b. 14.225

    c. 1,422.5

4. 3.336×6.2

    a. 2.06832

    b. 20.6832

    c. 206.832

Estimate the product.

5. $\$6.34 \times 8 = $ _____

6. $84.8 \times 5.6 = $ _____

7. $1.4 \times 7.7 = $ _____

8. $3.4 \times 87.3 = $ _____

9. $46.9 \times 1.8 = $ _____

10. $8.06 \times 8.9 = $ _____

11. $4.7 \times 96.2 = $ _____

12. $76.3 \times 2.4 = $ _____

13. $6.8 \times 1.9 = $ _____

14. $37.21 \times 49.9 = $ ____

15. $22.03 \times 198.2 = $ _____

16. $0.5 \times 1.07 = $ _____

17. $\$53.25 \times 16 = $ ____

18. $23.7 \times 18.76 = $ _____

19. $36.9 \times 170 = $ _____

Real World Connection

Write the number sentence and solve.

20. A board costs $3.63. How much do 236 boards cost?

_____

Name _____   Date _____

• • • • • • • • • • • • TIME TO WORK • • • • • • • • • • • •

 Estimate to place the decimal point in the product.

1. $6.8 \times 3.4 = 2\ 3\ 1\ 2$

2. $2.56 \times 4.6 = 1\ 1\ 7\ 7\ 6$

3. $6.787 \times 7.6 = 5\ 1\ 5\ 8\ 1\ 2$

4. $0.98 \times 4.6 = 4\ 5\ 0\ 8$

5. $0.97 \times 0.76 = 0\ 7\ 3\ 7\ 2$

6. $3.761 \times 0.5 = 1\ 8\ 8\ 0\ 5$

7.	**8.**	**9.**	**10.**
34.45	69	4.343	78.3
× 3.3	× 4.7	× 0.8	× 234
1 1 3 6 8 5	3 2 4 3	3 4 7 4 4	1 8 3 2 2 2

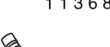 Find the product. Round money amounts to the nearest cent.

11.	**12.**	**13.**	**14.**
6.8	4.435	456.2	$25.98
× 3.4	× 5.6	× 3.5	× 6.7

15.	**16.**	**17.**	**18.**
68.77	$14.87	$674.65	$523.78
× 28	× 0.9	× 9.4	× 0.5

19. $15.8 \times 54 = $ _____

20. $\$125.65 \times 3.7 = $ _____

21. $6.89 \times 45 = $ _____

22. $543.2 \times 0.25 = $ _____

23. $7,965 \times 4.315 = $ _____

24. $1.5 \times 0.065 = $ _____

Real World Connection

Write the number sentence and solve.

25. Leon makes $5.65 an hour. How much did he make last week if he worked 39.5 hours?

_____

Multiplication of Whole Numbers and Decimals: Multiplying Decimals

Name _____ Date _____

• • • • • • • • • • PRODUCING ZEROS • • • • • • • • •

Place the decimal point in the product. Write zeros where necessary.

1. 0.02
× 3.6
7 2

2. 0.003
× 22.7
6 8 1

3. 0.098
× 4.1
4 0 1 8

4. 1.98
× 0.5
9 9 0

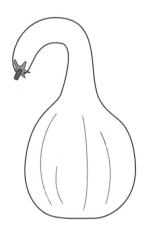

Find the product.

5. 0.078
× 9

6. 45.99
× 20.6

7. 0.07
× 6

8. 34.79
× 0.05

9. 0.67
× 507

10. 0.098
× 0.6

11. 0.0045
× 669

12. 8.7
× 0.6

13. 0.37
× 3.78

14. 0.002
× 60.4

15. 6.213
× 19

16. 29.1
× 0.02

17. $5.7 \times 100 =$ _____ **18.** $0.081 \times 10 =$ _____ **19.** $0.086 \times 1{,}000 =$ _____

20. $0.956 \times 100 =$ _____ **21.** $17.8 \times 1{,}000 =$ _____ **22.** $456.9 \times 10 =$ _____

Real World Connection

Write the number sentence and solve.

23. Apples costs $3.99 a pound. To the nearest cent, how much will 2.05 pounds cost?

_____

Multiplication of Whole Numbers and Decimals: Zeros in Products

Name _____ Date _____

·········· PRODUCT-TION PRACTICE ··········

 Estimate the product.

1. 23
   × 15

2. 301
   × 46

3. 5.8
   × 0.7

4. 53.2
   × 16

5. 36.9
   × 4.8

6. $4.67
   × 347

 Find the product. Round money amounts to the nearest cent.

7. 89
   × 8

8. 609
   × 83

9. $5.88
   × 9

10. 0.0004
    × 35

11. 9.345
    × 512

12. 0.06
    × 0.21

13. 2,381
    × 39

14. 558
    × 462

15. $8 \times 92 =$ _____

16. $\$3.67 \times 42 =$ _____

17. $49 \times 0.06 =$ _____

18. $135 \times 105 =$ _____

19. $4.68 \times 2.95 =$ _____

20. $2,005 \times 99 =$ _____

Real World Connection

Write the number sentence and solve.

21. Students rehearsed 5 weeks for the school play. They
practiced 15.5 hours each week. How many hours did
the students rehearse altogether?

_____

Multiplication of Whole Numbers and Decimals: Practice

Name _____   Date _____

···· VACATION TIMES PROBLEM SOLVING ····

Solve.

1. Karen's family bought 14 rolls of film for their vacation. There are 24 pictures on each roll of film. If they used all except 3 rolls, how many pictures did they take?

_____

2. Jill took a bike tour of France. She rode her bike 18.75 miles each day. After 7 days, how many miles had Jill ridden?

_____

3. A bus tour will cover 450 miles each day for 5 days. How many miles will the bus travel?

_____

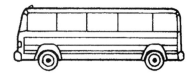

4. One travel agency is advertising round-trip airline tickets for $138.75. They book 56 tickets in one week. How much do these tickets cost altogether?

_____

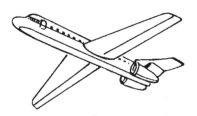

5. A travel poster is 0.0048 centimeters thick. How thick is a stack of 6 travel posters?

_____

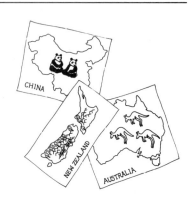

Multiplication of Whole Numbers and Decimals: Word Problems

·········· COOKING UP QUOTIENTS ··········

 Choose the best estimate. Circle **a**, **b**, or **c**.

1. 7)356   **a.** 50   **b.** 70   **c.** 25

2. 17)15,230   **a.** 2,000   **b.** 1,000   **c.** 3,000

3. 6,435 ÷ 34   **a.** 2,000   **b.** 200   **c.** 300

4. 612 ÷ 27   **a.** 20   **b.** 200   **c.** 30

 Estimate the quotient.

5. 756 ÷ 5   **6.** 570 ÷ 3   **7.** 4,235 ÷ 7   **8.** 3,981 ÷ 8

_____ _____ _____ _____

9. 425 ÷ 9   **10.** 7,765 ÷ 9   **11.** 786 ÷ 36   **12.** 7,267 ÷ 353

_____ _____ _____ _____

13. 15)25,782   **14.** 20)4,254   **15.** 37)612

16. 75)5,672   **17.** 48)7,920   **18.** 9)3,429

19. 8)5,735   **20.** 83)737   **21.** 59)4,453

Real World Connection

Write the number sentence and solve.

22. Mrs. Yamato is a cook. She needs to bake enough muffins to serve 350 people. If each pan holds 12 muffins, about how many pans of muffins must she bake?

_____

Division of Whole Numbers and Decimals: Estimating Quotients of Whole Numbers

Name _____ Date _____

•••••••••• DIVIDED DELIVERY ••••••••••

Find the quotient.

1. 6)96
16
−6
26
26

2. 5)265
53
25
15
15

3. 3)9,144
3048
−9
014
−12

4. 5)412
82 r.2
−40
012
−10
2

5. 9)15,255

6. 3)618

7. 3)294

8. 6)18,342

9. 5)78,278

10. 9)5,886

11. 502 ÷ 4 = _____

12. 9,244 ÷ 4 = _____

13. 1,737 ÷ 5 = _____

14. 57,321 ÷ 9 = _____

15. 24,626 ÷ 7 = _____

16. 26,424 ÷ 6 = _____

Real World Connection

Write the number sentence and solve.

17. A newsstand receives a delivery of 3,661 magazines in 7 cartons. The same number of magazines is in each carton. How many magazines are in one carton?

_____

Division of Whole Numbers and Decimals: Dividing with 1-Digit Divisors

Name _____   Date _____

 Find the quotient.

1. 83)‾598‾

2. 34)‾136‾

3. 81)‾648‾

4. 91)‾743‾

5. 73)‾3,504‾

6. 98)‾1,959‾

7. 33)‾12,837‾

8. 72)‾3,468‾

9. 25)‾1,825‾

10. 29)‾38,190‾

11. 265 ÷ 53 = _____

12. 129 ÷ 21 = _____

13. 5,396 ÷ 71 = _____

14. 2,066 ÷ 33 = _____

15. 2,618 ÷ 119 = _____

16. 5,865 ÷ 345 = _____

Real World Connection

Write the number sentence and solve.

17. Bill has 180 marbles. He puts 27 marbles in each bag.
How many bags does he fill?

_____

Division of Whole Numbers and Decimals: Dividing by 2-Digit Divisors

• • • • • • • • THE "WRITE" TO DIVIDE • • • • • • • • •

Find the quotient.

1. 9)3,609   **2.** 8)2,560

3. 6)9,600   **4.** 3)6,211

5. 14)4,231   **6.** 24)4,900   **7.** 67)23,452

8. 33)2,977   **9.** 18)1,926   **10.** 56)16,856

Use inverse operations to complete the tables.

	Divisor	Dividend	Quotient
11.	35	21,140	_____
12.	_____	5,025	1,005
13.	6	_____	80 r2

	Divisor	Dividend	Quotient
14.	63	12,852	_____
15.	27	_____	208
16.	_____	604	50 r4

Real World Connection

Write the number sentence and solve.

17. Masalina's store sold 480 pencils. In all, 80 boxes of pencils were sold. If the number of pencils in each box was the same, how many pencils were in each box?

_____

Division of Whole Numbers and Decimals: Zeros in Quotients

Name _____   Date _____

"WEIGHT" FOR THE POINT

Find the quotient.

1. 4)12.8

2. 8)13.76

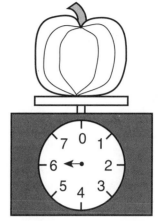

3. 7)26.6

4. 50.4 ÷ 12

Place the decimal point in the quotient.

5. 30.16 ÷ 13 = 2 3 2

6. 2.08 ÷ 8 = 0 2 6

7. 86.4 ÷ 27 = 3 2

Find the quotient.

8. 6)14.76

9. 11)11.88

10. 4)2.184

11. 9)4.158

12. 8)68.16

13. 29)152.25

14. 3.478 ÷ 74 = _____

15. 47.61 ÷ 23 = _____

16. 263.5 ÷ 5 = _____

Real World Connection

Write the number sentence and solve.

17. The total weight of 5 apples is 3.75 pounds. If each apple weighs about the same, about how much does each apple weigh?

_____

Division with Whole Numbers and Decimals: Dividing Decimals by Whole Numbers

Name _____   Date _____

• • • • • • • • • *THE POINT OF RUNNING* • • • • • • • • •

┌───┐
│ Divide until the remainder is zero. │
└───┘

1. 6)‾77.1‾   **2.** 8)‾20.76‾

3. 4)‾33.7‾   **4.** 8)‾5.2‾

5. 4)‾28.7‾   **6.** 5)‾1.58‾   **7.** 12)‾71.4‾

8. 28)‾207.34‾   **9.** 16)‾59.6‾   **10.** 24)‾12.12‾

11. 2.92 ÷ 8 = _____   **12.** 6.276 ÷ 6 = _____   **13.** 27.36 ÷ 60 = _____

┌──┐
│ **Real World Connection**   │
│    │
│ **Write the number sentence and solve.**   │
│ **14.** John can run 4 miles in 21 minutes. How long does   │
│ it take him to run 1 mile?   │
│   │
│ _____   │
└──┘

Division with Whole Numbers and Decimals: Dividing with No Remainders

Math 6, SV 8099-5

Name _____   Date _____

• • • • • • • • • • • • WORK TO DIVIDE • • • • • • • • • • • •

Place the decimal point in the quotient. Add zeros if necessary.

1. $32.85 \div 4.5 = 7\ 3$

2. $2.08 \div 0.8 = 2\ 6$

3. $368.48 \div 9.8 = 3\ 7\ 6$

4. $0.115 \div 2.3 = \qquad 5$

5. $39.52 \div 5.2 = 7\ 6$

6. $27.307 \div 8.3 = 3\ 2\ 9$

Find the quotient.

7. $0.72\overline{)31.32}$

8. $6.3\overline{)340.2}$

9. $2.1\overline{)8.841}$

10. $3.6\overline{)23.958}$

11. $0.11\overline{)496.1}$

12. $0.122\overline{)0.793}$

13. $2.38 \div 0.07$

14. $89.6 \div 0.16$

15. $0.2368 \div 0.37$

16. $86.36 \div 34$

17. $0.1449 \div 0.045$

18. $58.42 \div 0.23$

Real World Connection

Write the number sentence and solve.

19. Joanne earns $6.30 an hour. Last week she earned $232.47. For how many hours did she work?

_____

Division of Whole Numbers and Decimals: Dividing Decimals by Decimals

Math 6, SV 8099-5

Name _____   Date _____

•••••••••••• *SHOPPING AROUND* ••••••••••••

 Find the quotient. Round to the nearest whole number or dollar.

1. $2.70 ÷ 2 = _____   **2.** 33.2 ÷ 4.7 = _____

3. 20.6 ÷ 7 = _____   **4.** 116 ÷ 3 = _____

 Find the quotient. Round to the given place.

5. 18)‾20.2‾ _____   **6.** 7)‾$4.56‾ _____   **7.** 1.9)‾4.566‾ _____
       (tenths)   (cents)   (hundredths)

8. 4)‾1.71‾ _____   **9.** 2.6)‾7.43‾ _____   **10.** 6.6)‾15.8‾ _____
       (tenths)   (thousandths)   (hundredths)

11. $28.82 ÷ 4 = _____   **12.** 5.082 ÷ 4 = _____   **13.** 104.58 ÷ 2.5 = _____
    (hundredths)   (tenths)   (hundredths)

14. 26.1 ÷ 18 = _____   **15.** 145.8 ÷ 4.5 = _____   **16.** $6.67 ÷ 8 = _____
     (tenths)   (ones)   (hundredths)

Real World Connection

Write a number sentence and solve.

17. At the local market, 6 packs of gum sell for $2.22.
What is the cost of one pack of gum?

_____

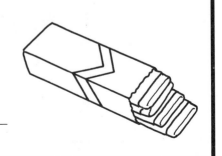

•••••••••••• RECYCLED PRACTICE ••••••••••••

Find the quotient.

1. $34\overline{)136}$

2. $8\overline{)669}$

3. $4\overline{)28.8}$

4. $73\overline{)3,508}$

5. $94\overline{)85,164}$

6. $.06\overline{)5.082}$

7. $1.45\overline{)36.25}$

8. $648 \div 8 =$ _____

9. $4.2 \div 5 =$ _____

10. $3.7 \div .2 =$ _____

11. $13.455 \div 6.5 =$ _____

12. $2,266 \div 11 =$ _____

13. $104.25 \div 2.5 =$ _____

Real World Connection

Write the number sentence and solve.

14. A recycling company recycled 68.1 tons of aluminum in 5 months. If the company recycled the same amount each month, how many tons of aluminum did it recycle monthly?

_____

Division of Whole Numbers and Decimals: Practice

Math 6, SV 8099-5

Name _____   Date _____

••••• THE CRAFT OF PROBLEM SOLVING •••••

 Solve.

1. Janet receives a box with 598 vases. How many vases can she put on 7 shelves if she puts the same number on each shelf?

_____

2. Kevin is framing a picture. He bought 4 pieces of framing for a total of $6.52. How much was each piece of wood?

_____

3. A book company ships 1,825 sewing books. If 25 books fit in a box, how many boxes does the company ship?

_____

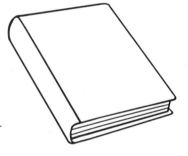

4. At ABC Craft Supply, the cost of 6 tubes of paint is $8.34. Sharon has only $3.00. How many tubes can she buy with this money? How much money will she have left over?

_____

5. A crafts store sells two brands of embroidery floss. Brand A costs $2.64 for 12 skeins. Brand B sells for $0.28 a skein. Which brand is the better buy?

_____

Division of Whole Numbers and Decimals: Word Problems

Name _____ Date _____

•••••••••• FRUITFUL NUMBERS ••••••••••

Write the first three multiples, excluding the number itself.

1. 4   **2.** 8   **3.** 13

_____   _____   _____

4. 18   **5.** 19   **6.** 7

_____   _____   _____

Find the LCM for each group of numbers.

7. 8, 20   **8.** 2, 18   **9.** 4, 7   **10.** 7, 9

_____   _____   _____   _____

11. 6, 15   **12.** 3, 8   **13.** 12, 16   **14.** 15, 25

_____   _____   _____   _____

15. 20, 25   **16.** 25, 120   **17.** 2, 3, 4   **18.** 3, 4, 24

_____   _____   _____   _____

19. 12, 15, 20   **20.** 16, 24, 32   **21.** 15, 20, 80   **22.** 9, 11, 33

_____   _____   _____   _____

Real World Connection

Solve.

23. Donald wants to buy the same number of apples and pears. Apples are sold in packages of 4 and pears are sold in packages of 7. What is the least number of apples he can buy?

_____

Fractions: Least Common Multiples

Name _____   Date _____

 ·············· **EQUAL AMOUNTS** ··············

 Write a fraction that tells what part is shaded.

1.

2.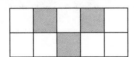

3.

_____   _____   _____

Write the equivalent fraction.

4. $\frac{1}{4} = \frac{\square}{20}$

5. $\frac{1}{6} = \frac{6}{\square}$

6. $\frac{3}{6} = \frac{15}{\square}$

7. $\frac{4}{9} = \frac{\square}{27}$

8. $\frac{10}{12} = \frac{\square}{6}$

9. $\frac{18}{42} = \frac{3}{\square}$

10. $\frac{20}{45} = \frac{\square}{9}$

11. $\frac{27}{45} = \frac{3}{\square}$

12. $\frac{2}{3} = \frac{\square}{9}$

13. $\frac{1}{5} = \frac{\square}{10}$

14. $\frac{6}{12} = \frac{1}{\square}$

15. $\frac{3}{8} = \frac{12}{\square}$

Write yes or no to tell whether the fractions are equivalent.
If they are not, write an equivalent fraction for each fraction.

16. $\frac{3}{4}, \frac{15}{20}$

17. $\frac{7}{14}, \frac{20}{28}$

18. $\frac{2}{5}, \frac{4}{12}$

19. $\frac{4}{7}, \frac{20}{35}$

_____   _____   _____   _____

Real World Connection

Solve.

20. Cory answered 6 questions out of 8 correct on his last
quiz. How many questions must he answer correctly
to get the same score on a quiz with 24 questions?

_____

Fractions: Equivalent Fractions

Math 6, SV 8099-5

Name _____   Date _____

•••••••••••• FRACTIONAL VOTING ••••••••••••

Solve.

1. Find common multiples   4:   4   8   12   16   20   24
   of 4 and 6. _____   6:   6   12   18   24   30   36

   What are two common denominators for $\frac{1}{4}$ and $\frac{5}{6}$? _____

2. Find common multiples   2:   2   4   6   8   10
   of 2 and 4. _____   4:   4   8   12   16   20

   What are two common denominators of $\frac{1}{2}$ and $\frac{1}{4}$? _____

Write each pair of fractions by using the LCD.

3. $\frac{1}{4}$, $\frac{5}{6}$

   _____

4. $\frac{1}{2}$, $\frac{1}{4}$

   _____

5. $\frac{2}{5}$, $\frac{3}{10}$

   _____

6. $\frac{3}{4}$, $\frac{1}{8}$

   _____

7. $\frac{2}{5}$, $\frac{1}{6}$

   _____

8. $\frac{3}{8}$, $\frac{1}{12}$

   _____

9. $\frac{4}{7}$, $\frac{3}{14}$

   _____

10. $\frac{3}{4}$, $\frac{2}{9}$

   _____

11. $\frac{1}{9}$, $\frac{2}{3}$

   _____

12. $\frac{5}{6}$, $\frac{3}{8}$

   _____

13. $\frac{4}{9}$, $\frac{2}{18}$

   _____

14. $\frac{3}{7}$, $\frac{2}{6}$

   _____

Real World Connection

Solve.

15. In an election, $\frac{3}{8}$ of the voters voted for Candidate A, and $\frac{5}{16}$ of the voters voted for Candidate B. What is the LCD for the two fractions?

   _____

Fraction: Least Common Denominators

Name _____ Date _____

 Use <, >, or = to compare the fractions.

1. $\frac{1}{4}$ ◯ $\frac{3}{8}$ 2. $\frac{1}{3}$ ◯ $\frac{5}{6}$

3. $\frac{3}{4}$ ◯ $\frac{5}{12}$ 4. $\frac{1}{5}$ ◯ $\frac{2}{25}$

5. $\frac{3}{7}$ ◯ $\frac{2}{5}$ 6. $\frac{5}{6}$ ◯ $\frac{2}{9}$ 7. $\frac{1}{10}$ ◯ $\frac{2}{15}$ 8. $\frac{5}{8}$ ◯ $\frac{7}{12}$

9. $\frac{3}{5}$ ◯ $\frac{4}{5}$ 10. $\frac{2}{3}$ ◯ $\frac{3}{5}$ 11. $\frac{5}{12}$ ◯ $\frac{4}{6}$ 12. $\frac{4}{15}$ ◯ $\frac{3}{12}$

13. $\frac{15}{32}$ ◯ $\frac{6}{16}$ 14. $\frac{5}{10}$ ◯ $\frac{3}{6}$ 15. $\frac{10}{14}$ ◯ $\frac{15}{21}$ 16. $\frac{15}{25}$ ◯ $\frac{25}{50}$

 Write in order from least to greatest. Use <.

17. $\frac{2}{15}, \frac{1}{5}, \frac{3}{5}$ 18. $\frac{2}{3}, \frac{3}{4}, \frac{1}{8}$ 19. $\frac{2}{5}, \frac{2}{3}, \frac{1}{2}$

_____   _____   _____

20. $\frac{5}{6}, \frac{2}{3}, \frac{3}{8}$ 21. $\frac{1}{3}, \frac{1}{2}, \frac{5}{9}$ 22. $\frac{2}{6}, \frac{3}{12}, \frac{3}{4}$

_____   _____   _____

Real World Connection

Solve.

23. For English class, Mary Ann had read $\frac{2}{3}$ of the books on the reading list. Jesse had read $\frac{5}{6}$ of the books. Alan had read $\frac{3}{4}$ of the books. Who read the most books?

_____

Fractions: Comparing and Ordering Fractions

Name _____   Date _____

·········· A PRIME GARDEN SPOT ··········

 Tell whether each number is prime or composite.

1. 13 _____   **2.** 18 _____

3. 45 _____   **4.** 53 _____

 Write the factors of each number.

5. 8 _____   **6.** 15 _____   **7.** 10 _____

8. 50 _____   **9.** 35 _____   **10.** 28 _____

11. 40 _____   **12.** 65 _____   **13.** 77 _____

Use a factor tree. Write the prime factorization.

14. 20 _____   **15.** 75 _____   **16.** 63 _____

Real World Connection

Solve.

17. Rita has 48 flowers to plant in her garden. If each row in her garden must have the same number of flowers, what different arrangements can Rita make?

_____

_____

Fractions: Factors, Primes, and Composites

Math 6, SV 8099-5

Name _____ Date _____

FACTOR-Y WORK

Write the common factors of each pair of numbers.

1. 16, 30 _____   2. 12, 18 _____

3. 24, 30 _____   4. 15, 45 _____

5. 20, 30 _____   6. 15, 20 _____

Write the GCF of each pair of numbers.

7. 8, 10 _____   8. 16, 18 _____   9. 7, 21 _____

10. 54, 9 _____   11. 15, 20 _____   12. 12, 8 _____

13. 15, 45 _____   14. 48, 6 _____   15. 30, 24 _____

16. 9, 21 _____   17. 12, 15 _____   18. 18, 36 _____

Real World Connection

Solve.

19. Samantha has two pieces of cloth. One piece is 72 inches wide and the other piece is 90 inches wide. She wants to cut both pieces into strips of equal width that are as wide as possible. How wide should she cut the strips?

_____

Fractions: Greatest Common Factors

Name _____   Date _____

Write the GCF of the numerator and denominator.

1. $\frac{10}{15}$ _____ 2. $\frac{12}{16}$ _____ 3. $\frac{6}{14}$ _____

4. $\frac{36}{50}$ _____ 5. $\frac{30}{60}$ _____ 6. $\frac{25}{40}$ _____

7. $\frac{9}{24}$ _____ 8. $\frac{8}{48}$ _____ 9. $\frac{24}{32}$ _____

Write the fraction in simplest form.

10. $\frac{15}{25}$ _____ 11. $\frac{14}{21}$ _____ 12. $\frac{6}{15}$ _____ 13. $\frac{7}{14}$ _____

14. $\frac{35}{45}$ _____ 15. $\frac{18}{36}$ _____ 16. $\frac{45}{50}$ _____ 17. $\frac{7}{35}$ _____

18. $\frac{16}{48}$ _____ 19. $\frac{15}{24}$ _____ 20. $\frac{16}{16}$ _____ 21. $\frac{32}{40}$ _____

Circle the fraction that is in simplest form.

22. $\frac{4}{12}$, $\frac{3}{6}$, $\frac{4}{5}$, $\frac{3}{9}$ 23. $\frac{2}{7}$, $\frac{3}{6}$, $\frac{4}{16}$, $\frac{9}{12}$ 24. $\frac{8}{12}$, $\frac{6}{27}$, $\frac{7}{21}$, $\frac{8}{15}$

25. $\frac{3}{24}$, $\frac{4}{13}$, $\frac{2}{6}$, $\frac{3}{6}$ 26. $\frac{5}{12}$, $\frac{3}{9}$, $\frac{25}{75}$, $\frac{36}{48}$ 27. $\frac{10}{25}$, $\frac{11}{15}$, $\frac{12}{27}$, $\frac{14}{32}$

Real World Connection

Solve.

28. There are 12 girls and 8 boys in Mr. Frank's art class. What part of the class is girls?

_____

Fractions: Simplest Form

Name _____ Date _____

COOKIE MIXES

Find the missing digits.

1. $\dfrac{7}{3} = 2\dfrac{1}{\boxed{}}$

2. $\dfrac{29}{6} = \boxed{}\dfrac{5}{6}$

3. $\dfrac{38}{5} = \boxed{}\dfrac{3}{5}$

4. $9\dfrac{2}{3} = \dfrac{\boxed{}}{3}$

5. $\dfrac{30}{7} = \boxed{}\dfrac{2}{7}$

6. $\dfrac{14}{5} = 2\dfrac{\boxed{}}{5}$

Write the fraction as a mixed number or as a whole number.

7. $\dfrac{41}{8}$ _____

8. $\dfrac{7}{3}$ _____

9. $\dfrac{29}{11}$ _____

10. $\dfrac{15}{4}$ _____

11. $\dfrac{27}{3}$ _____

12. $\dfrac{76}{12}$ _____

13. $\dfrac{81}{3}$ _____

14. $\dfrac{37}{5}$ _____

Write the mixed number as a fraction.

15. $9\dfrac{1}{7}$ _____

16. $5\dfrac{7}{9}$ _____

17. $2\dfrac{3}{4}$ _____

18. $6\dfrac{2}{7}$ _____

19. $3\dfrac{3}{8}$ _____

20. $1\dfrac{9}{10}$ _____

21. $8\dfrac{1}{8}$ _____

22. $6\dfrac{7}{11}$ _____

Real World Connection

Solve.

23. Joy bakes a double recipe of cookies. She calculates that she needs $\dfrac{10}{3}$ cups of flour. In simplest form, how much flour will Joy need to measure?

_____

Fractions: Mixed Numbers

Name _____ Date _____

··········"SUM" DIFFERENT ADDS··········

Round the fractions to 0, $\frac{1}{2}$, or 1. Then rewrite the problem.

1. $\frac{10}{11} + \frac{7}{9}$ _____

2. $6\frac{1}{3} - 4\frac{1}{4}$ _____

3. $\frac{7}{8} + \frac{1}{2}$ _____

4. $12\frac{6}{7} - 4\frac{4}{5}$ _____

5. $5\frac{1}{3} + 2\frac{1}{8}$ _____

6. $4\frac{2}{15} - 2\frac{3}{4}$ _____

Estimate the sum or difference.

7. $\frac{1}{16} + \frac{5}{8} =$ _____

8. $\frac{1}{7} + \frac{7}{9} =$ _____

9. $\frac{4}{5} - \frac{5}{9} =$ _____

10. $2\frac{4}{7} + 1\frac{2}{17} =$ _____

11. $\frac{12}{17} - \frac{1}{5} =$ _____

12. $10\frac{4}{5} - 3\frac{5}{9} =$ _____

13. $2\frac{3}{8} - 1\frac{1}{4} =$ _____

14. $\frac{14}{19} + \frac{1}{6} =$ _____

15. $2\frac{1}{5} + 3\frac{7}{8} =$ _____

16. $\frac{5}{6} - \frac{1}{15} =$ _____

17. $7\frac{1}{2} + 2\frac{4}{7} =$ _____

18. $8\frac{1}{5} - 4\frac{3}{4} =$ _____

Real World Connection

Solve.

19. Rogelio sold a $\frac{1}{3}$ page ad to client A, a $\frac{3}{4}$ page ad to client B, and a $\frac{1}{8}$ page ad to client C. Rogelio says he sold about $1\frac{1}{2}$ pages of ads. Is he right? Explain.

_____

Fractions: Estimating Sums and Differences

Math 6, SV 8099-5

Name _____ Date _____

Find the sum or difference. Write your answer in simplest form.

1. $\frac{3}{5} + \frac{1}{5} =$ _____

2. $\frac{8}{9} - \frac{2}{9} =$ _____

3. $\frac{3}{10} + \frac{2}{10} =$ _____

4. $\frac{4}{12} - \frac{2}{12} =$ _____

5. $\frac{3}{8} + \frac{4}{8} =$ _____

6. $\frac{4}{6} - \frac{2}{6} =$ _____

7. $\frac{8}{12} + \frac{1}{12} =$ _____

8. $\frac{6}{7} - \frac{5}{7} =$ _____

9. $\frac{1}{14} + \frac{6}{14} =$ _____

10. $\frac{5}{8} - \frac{3}{8} =$ _____

11. $\frac{6}{9} + \frac{2}{9} =$ _____

12. $\frac{14}{15} - \frac{8}{15} =$ _____

13. $\frac{6}{7} - \frac{2}{7} =$ _____

14. $\frac{3}{9} + \frac{4}{9} =$ _____

15. $\frac{4}{10} - \frac{1}{10} =$ _____

16. $\frac{1}{4} + \frac{3}{4} =$ _____

17. $\frac{5}{6} - \frac{3}{6} =$ _____

18. $\frac{5}{12} + \frac{1}{12} =$ _____

Real World Connection

Write the number sentence and solve.

19. Dina lives $\frac{9}{10}$ mile from the park. If she has ridden her bike $\frac{4}{10}$ mile, how much farther does she have to ride?

_____

Fractions: Adding and Subtracting Like Fractions

Name _____ Date _____

Write the equivalent fraction by finding the missing digits.

1. $\frac{2}{3} = \dfrac{\boxed{}}{12}$

   $+\frac{1}{4} = \dfrac{\boxed{}}{12}$
   _____
   $\dfrac{\boxed{}}{12}$

2. $\frac{4}{5} = \dfrac{8}{\boxed{}}$

   $-\frac{1}{2} = \dfrac{5}{\boxed{}}$
   _____
   $\dfrac{3}{\boxed{}}$

Find the sum or difference. Write your answer in simplest form.

3. $\frac{1}{2}$
   $+\frac{1}{8}$

4. $\frac{4}{5}$
   $-\frac{2}{3}$

5. $\frac{2}{6}$
   $+\frac{3}{10}$

6. $\frac{3}{4}$
   $-\frac{3}{8}$

7. $\frac{2}{5}$
   $+\frac{2}{4}$

8. $\frac{2}{5}$
   $-\frac{2}{6}$

9. $\frac{2}{3}$
   $+\frac{4}{5}$

10. $\frac{5}{6}$
   $-\frac{1}{3}$

Real World Connection

Write the number sentence and solve.

11. Whit usually drives $\frac{3}{4}$ mile to work on the expressway. When the traffic is bad he takes another route that is $\frac{7}{8}$ mile long. How much shorter is his usual route?

_____

Fractions: Adding and Subtracting Unlike Fractions

Math 6, SV 8099-5

Name _____ Date _____

···· AMUSEMENT PARK ADD-TRACTIONS ····

| Find the sum. Write your answer in simplest form. |

1. $4\frac{5}{12}$
    $+ 3\frac{2}{12}$

2. $8\frac{1}{10}$
    $+ 1\frac{7}{10}$

3. $5\frac{2}{5}$
    $+ 2\frac{1}{15}$

4. $1\frac{5}{9}$
    $+ 2\frac{1}{3}$

5. $8\frac{2}{3}$
    $+ 7\frac{3}{7}$

6. $4\frac{3}{8}$
    $+ 3\frac{3}{4}$

7. $7\frac{3}{10}$
    $+ 7\frac{5}{10}$

8. $2\frac{1}{9}$
    $+ 5\frac{5}{9}$

9. $3\frac{3}{13}$
    $+ 2\frac{5}{13}$

10. $3\frac{4}{8}$
     $+ 9\frac{2}{8}$

11. $1\frac{2}{6}$
     $+ 8\frac{3}{6}$

12. $4\frac{11}{15}$
     $+ 5\frac{2}{3}$

13. $12\frac{2}{3}$
     $+ 4\frac{2}{9}$

14. $5\frac{1}{3}$
     $+ 4\frac{3}{8}$

15. $3\frac{6}{7}$
     $+ 4\frac{1}{4}$

16. $4\frac{1}{2}$
     $+ 3\frac{1}{3}$

17. $14\frac{2}{5} + 3\frac{1}{3} = $_____

18. $11\frac{4}{9} + 8\frac{1}{4} = $_____

19. $17\frac{2}{9} + 2\frac{5}{8} = $_____

Real World Connection

Write the number sentence and solve.

20. Jan worked in the amusement park $4\frac{2}{5}$ hours on
Friday and $6\frac{3}{10}$ hours on Saturday. How many hours
did Jan work in all?

_____

Fractions: Adding Mixed Numbers

Math 6, SV 8099-5

Name _____ Date _____

·············· MIXING UP PAINT ··············

Tell whether or not you must rename the larger number.
Then rename if necessary.

1. $3\frac{2}{7} - 1\frac{5}{7} =$ _____   2. $5\frac{6}{10} - 2\frac{2}{10} =$ _____

3. $4\frac{7}{8} - 3\frac{1}{8} =$ _____   4. $1\frac{3}{11} - \frac{6}{11} =$ _____

Rename the larger number.

5. $3 - 1\frac{3}{5} =$ _____   6. $3\frac{1}{7} - 1\frac{2}{7} =$ _____

7. $6 - 2\frac{3}{4} =$ _____   8. $7\frac{3}{13} - 5\frac{7}{13} =$ _____

Find the difference. Write the answer in simplest form.

9. $\begin{aligned}15\frac{4}{5}\\-2\frac{1}{5}\end{aligned}$ 10. $\begin{aligned}6\frac{1}{7}\\-1\frac{3}{7}\end{aligned}$ 11. $\begin{aligned}8\frac{3}{15}\\-5\frac{2}{15}\end{aligned}$ 12. $\begin{aligned}6\\-4\frac{10}{11}\end{aligned}$ 13. $\begin{aligned}9\frac{2}{13}\\-5\frac{5}{13}\end{aligned}$

14. $\begin{aligned}8\frac{17}{18}\\-6\frac{5}{18}\end{aligned}$ 15. $\begin{aligned}3\frac{1}{5}\\-1\frac{3}{5}\end{aligned}$ 16. $\begin{aligned}6\frac{4}{9}\\-4\frac{5}{9}\end{aligned}$ 17. $\begin{aligned}10\frac{7}{15}\\-8\frac{4}{15}\end{aligned}$ 18. $\begin{aligned}17\frac{6}{10}\\-9\frac{3}{10}\end{aligned}$

Real World Connection

Write the number sentence and solve.

19. An art class made yellow paint by mixing $5\frac{7}{8}$ jars of
blue paint and $3\frac{3}{8}$ jars of green paint. How many
more jars of blue paint than yellow paint were used?

_____

Fractions: Subtracting Mixed Numbers with Like Denominators

Math 6, SV 8099-5

Name _____   Date _____

•••••• WRESTLING WITH FRACTIONS ••••••

Find the difference.

1. $8\frac{5}{6}$
$-3\frac{1}{3}$

2. $8\frac{3}{7}$
$-3\frac{1}{4}$

3. $5\frac{6}{10}$
$-1\frac{1}{5}$

4. $7\frac{2}{3}$
$-2\frac{1}{4}$

5. $9\frac{3}{7}$
$-2\frac{1}{2}$

6. $8\frac{1}{6}$
$-2\frac{2}{3}$

7. $19\frac{1}{5}$
$-12\frac{2}{3}$

8. $21\frac{4}{7}$
$-16\frac{1}{3}$

9. $27\frac{1}{3}$
$-12\frac{3}{8}$

10. $33\frac{1}{2}$
$-22\frac{5}{6}$

11. $45\frac{2}{3}$
$-25\frac{9}{10}$

12. $14\frac{1}{5} - 3\frac{2}{15} = $ _____

13. $18\frac{3}{4} - 12\frac{7}{9} = $ _____

14. $35\frac{1}{2} - 31\frac{4}{7} = $ _____

15. $5\frac{1}{7} - 2\frac{3}{4} = $ _____

16. $8\frac{1}{3} - 4\frac{1}{5} = $ _____

17. $4\frac{8}{9} - 1\frac{1}{2} = $ _____

Real World Connection

Write the number sentence and solve.

18. Clint is a wrestler who weighs $143\frac{1}{4}$ pounds. His opponent weighs $141\frac{1}{2}$ pounds. By how much does Clint outweigh his opponent?

_____

Fractions: Subtracting Mixed Numbers with Unlike Denominators

Math 6, SV 8099-5

Name _____ Date _____

 Complete the multiplication sentence. Write the product in simplest form.

1. $\frac{2}{4} \times \frac{2}{3} =$ _____   2. $\frac{5}{6} \times \frac{2}{3} =$ _____

 Solve. Write the product in simplest form.

3. $\frac{1}{4} \times \frac{1}{5} =$ _____   4. $\frac{1}{4} \times \frac{1}{4} =$ _____   5. $\frac{1}{5} \times \frac{2}{7} =$ _____   6. $\frac{1}{2} \times \frac{5}{6} =$ _____

7. $\frac{3}{8} \times \frac{1}{5} =$ _____   8. $\frac{4}{5} \times \frac{1}{10} =$ _____   9. $\frac{3}{7} \times \frac{5}{6} =$ _____   10. $\frac{5}{6} \times \frac{6}{7} =$ _____

11. $\frac{2}{5} \times \frac{4}{7} =$ _____   12. $\frac{1}{9} \times \frac{2}{3} =$ _____   13. $\frac{4}{7} \times \frac{1}{12} =$ _____   14. $\frac{5}{9} \times \frac{9}{10} =$ _____

15. $\frac{3}{4} \times \frac{1}{6} =$ _____   16. $\frac{2}{3} \times \frac{5}{9} =$ _____   17. $\frac{3}{7} \times \frac{2}{5} =$ _____   18. $\frac{6}{7} \times \frac{7}{8} =$ _____

Real World Connection

Write the number sentence and solve.

19. One third of the students in Mrs. Monroe's class have pets. One half of these students have dogs. What part of the students have dogs?

_____

Fractions: Multiplying Fractions

Name _____ Date _____

• • • • • A SIMPLE "WEIGH" TO MULTIPLY • • • • •

 Simplify the factors.

1. $\frac{1}{3} \times \frac{3}{4}$ = _____

2. $\frac{1}{2} \times \frac{4}{7}$ = _____

3. $\frac{3}{7} \times \frac{5}{6}$ = _____

4. $\frac{3}{7} \times \frac{7}{9}$ = _____

5. $\frac{3}{5} \times \frac{2}{9}$ = _____

6. $\frac{5}{10} \times \frac{2}{3}$ = _____

7. $\frac{2}{3} \times \frac{9}{10}$ = _____

8. $\frac{4}{8} \times \frac{3}{4}$ = _____

9. $\frac{6}{8} \times \frac{2}{15}$ = _____

10. $\frac{3}{5} \times \frac{5}{6}$ = _____

11. $\frac{3}{4} \times \frac{12}{15}$ = _____

12. $\frac{4}{7} \times \frac{14}{16}$ = _____

13. $\frac{2}{18} \times \frac{9}{10}$ = _____

14. $\frac{5}{16} \times \frac{4}{15}$ = _____

 Choose a method. Find the product.
Write the product in simplest form.

15. $\frac{2}{3} \times \frac{3}{4}$ = _____

16. $\frac{4}{7} \times \frac{2}{8}$ = _____

17. $\frac{3}{10} \times \frac{5}{9}$ = _____

18. $\frac{6}{7} \times \frac{14}{15}$ = _____

19. $\frac{6}{12} \times \frac{2}{3}$ = _____

20. $\frac{5}{12} \times \frac{3}{11}$ = _____

21. $\frac{3}{16} \times \frac{4}{9}$ = _____

22. $\frac{7}{24} \times \frac{6}{14}$ = _____

23. $\frac{6}{11} \times \frac{22}{24}$ = _____

24. $\frac{5}{16} \times \frac{4}{15}$ = _____

25. $\frac{6}{10} \times \frac{15}{16}$ = _____

26. $\frac{5}{9} \times \frac{12}{15}$ = _____

27. $\frac{2}{13} \times \frac{2}{16}$ = _____

28. $\frac{3}{4} \times \frac{12}{15}$ = _____

29. $\frac{5}{12} \times \frac{24}{25}$ = _____

30. $\frac{5}{24} \times \frac{12}{15}$ = _____

Real World Connection

Write the number sentence to solve.

31. At Pizza Heaven, $\frac{5}{8}$ of the weight of a pizza is the toppings. Two-thirds of this weight is the cheese. What part of the entire pizza is the weight of the cheese?

_____

Fractions: Multiplying by Simplifying

Math 6, SV 8099-5

Name _____ Date _____

········ TAKING STOCK OF PRODUCTS ·······

 Use rounding to estimate the product.

1. $\frac{4}{5} \times \frac{2}{3} =$ _____ **2.** $\frac{5}{12} \times \frac{8}{9} =$ _____

3. $\frac{10}{11} \times \frac{4}{7} =$ _____ **4.** $\frac{6}{15} \times \frac{3}{5} =$ _____

Use compatible numbers to estimate the product.

5. $\frac{1}{3} \times 59 =$ _____ **6.** $\frac{1}{6} \times 373 =$ _____ **7.** $710 \times \frac{2}{3} =$ _____

8. $\frac{5}{6} \times 30 =$ _____ **9.** $\frac{2}{3} \times 16 =$ _____ **10.** $\frac{6}{11} \times 235 =$ _____

Tell whether the estimate is reasonable. Write _yes_ or _no_.

11. $\frac{1}{4} \times 405 \approx 100$ ____ **12.** $\frac{14}{15} \times \frac{7}{12} \approx \frac{1}{2}$ _____ **13.** $\frac{8}{17} \times 340 \approx 200$ _____

14. $\frac{4}{5} \times 678 \approx 750$ ____ **15.** $\frac{1}{3} \times 400 \approx 200$ _____ **16.** $\frac{3}{4} \times 807 \approx 600$ _____

17. $\frac{5}{6} \times 298 \approx 250$ ____ **18.** $\frac{7}{15} \times 300 \approx 100$ _____ **19.** $\frac{2}{3} \times 150 \approx 75$ _____

Real World Connection

Write the number sentence and solve.

20. At a sporting goods store, $\frac{3}{5}$ of the tennis rackets in stock are metal. If there are 52 tennis rackets in stock, about how many are metal?

_____

Fractions: Estimating Products

Name _____ Date _____

Write each mixed number as a fraction. Then simplify.

1. $1\frac{3}{4} \times \frac{4}{5}$ _____

2. $\frac{6}{7} \times 3\frac{2}{3}$ _____

3. $2\frac{1}{3} \times 1\frac{3}{5}$ _____

4. $1\frac{1}{6} \times 2\frac{12}{13}$ _____

Tell whether the product will be less than both factors, between the factors, or greater than both factors.

5. $\frac{1}{6} \times \frac{4}{5}$

6. $\frac{1}{8} \times 3\frac{1}{2}$

7. $\frac{4}{5} \times 2\frac{1}{6}$

_____ _____ _____

8. $2\frac{1}{7} \times 1\frac{4}{9}$

9. $1\frac{6}{14} \times \frac{1}{10}$

10. $\frac{4}{5} \times 1\frac{1}{2}$

_____ _____ _____

Find the product.

11. $4\frac{3}{4} \times 1\frac{1}{3} =$ _____

12. $1\frac{5}{6} \times 3\frac{1}{11} =$ _____

13. $4\frac{1}{2} \times 2\frac{2}{5} =$ _____

14. $7\frac{1}{8} \times 1\frac{2}{3} =$ _____

15. $3\frac{1}{6} \times 2\frac{2}{3} =$ _____

16. $1\frac{3}{4} \times 2\frac{4}{7} =$ _____

17. $10\frac{1}{3} \times 1\frac{1}{3} =$ _____

18. $3\frac{1}{7} \times 4\frac{9}{10} =$ _____

19. $3\frac{1}{5} \times 6\frac{1}{4} =$ _____

20. $\frac{8}{9} \times 3\frac{3}{4} =$ _____

21. $8\frac{4}{9} \times 1\frac{1}{4} =$ _____

22. $6\frac{2}{3} \times 3\frac{3}{4} =$ _____

Real World Connection

Write the number sentence and solve.

23. Mr. Phillips has $1\frac{2}{3}$ cups of fruit to make a salad. The fruit is $\frac{1}{4}$ oranges. How many cups of oranges does he have?

_____

········· DIVIDE MEANS MULTIPLY ·········

Write the reciprocal of the divisor.

1. $8 \div \frac{1}{3}$ _____   **2.** $6 \div \frac{2}{5}$ _____

3. $\frac{2}{3} \div 4$ _____   **4.** $\frac{4}{5} \div 5$ _____

5. $\frac{3}{4} \div \frac{2}{3}$ _____   **6.** $4 \div \frac{1}{7}$ _____

7. $5 \div \frac{2}{9}$ _____   **8.** $\frac{2}{5} \div \frac{3}{8}$ _____   **9.** $\frac{7}{8} \div \frac{1}{8}$ _____   **10.** $\frac{6}{11} \div \frac{5}{7}$ _____

11. $\frac{4}{7} \div \frac{3}{5}$ _____   **12.** $\frac{9}{10} \div \frac{1}{16}$ _____   **13.** $\frac{2}{3} \div \frac{2}{3}$ _____   **14.** $20 \div \frac{1}{20}$ _____

Find the multiplication sentence to find the quotient of the division sentence.

15. $\frac{2}{3} \div \frac{1}{5} =$ ____ $\frac{2}{3} \times$ ____ $=$ ____   **16.** $\frac{2}{3} \div \frac{1}{6} =$ ____ $\frac{2}{3} \times$ ____ $=$ ____

17. $\frac{5}{8} \div \frac{3}{4} =$ ____ $\frac{5}{8} \times$ ____ $=$ ____   **18.** $\frac{1}{7} \div \frac{2}{3} =$ ____ $\frac{1}{7} \times$ ____ $=$ ____

19. $\frac{4}{5} \div \frac{3}{7} =$ ____ $\frac{4}{5} \times$ ____ $=$ ____   **20.** $\frac{5}{6} \div \frac{1}{4} =$ ____ $\frac{5}{6} \times$ ____ $=$ ____

Real World Connection

Solve.

21. Ron incorrectly answered a test question. When given the equation $\frac{2}{3} \div 4$, he solved the problem by writing the reciprocal equation as $\frac{3}{2} \times \frac{1}{4}$. Explain why Ron's answer was wrong.

_____

Fractions: Reciprocals in Division

55

Name _____ Date _____

••••••••••• FRACTIONAL SERVINGS ••••••••••

 **Complete.**

1. $\frac{1}{3} \div \frac{1}{2} = \frac{1}{3} \times \frac{2}{1} = $ _____

2. $8 \div \frac{1}{4} = 8 \times$ _____ = _____

3. $4 \div \frac{4}{5} = $ _____ $\times \frac{5}{4} = $ _____

4. $\frac{1}{3} \div \frac{3}{5} = \frac{1}{3} \times$ _____ = _____

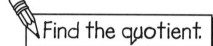 **Find the quotient.**

5. $10 \div \frac{4}{5} = $ _____

6. $5 \div \frac{2}{5} = $ _____

7. $\frac{2}{3} \div \frac{4}{7} = $ _____

8. $\frac{7}{8} \div \frac{1}{2} = $ _____

9. $9 \div \frac{3}{7} = $ _____

10. $12 \div \frac{3}{4} = $ _____

11. $\frac{3}{4} \div \frac{1}{12} = $ _____

12. $\frac{4}{7} \div \frac{3}{14} = $ _____

13. $6 \div \frac{3}{5} = $ _____

14. $\frac{9}{10} \div \frac{3}{7} = $ _____

15. $4 \div \frac{5}{6} = $ _____

16. $\frac{2}{5} \div \frac{3}{10} = $ _____

17. $\frac{2}{3} \div \frac{2}{5} = $ _____

18. $\frac{2}{5} \div \frac{1}{6} = $ _____

19. $\frac{5}{6} \div \frac{1}{2} = $ _____

20. $\frac{11}{9} \div \frac{8}{3} = $ _____

21. $\frac{1}{2} \div \frac{5}{8} = $ _____

22. $\frac{8}{9} \div \frac{1}{9} = $ _____

23. $\frac{4}{5} \div \frac{2}{5} = $ _____

24. $\frac{3}{5} \div \frac{3}{4} = $ _____

Real World Connection

Write the number sentence and solve.

25. Alex has $\frac{5}{6}$ can of popcorn. It takes $\frac{1}{8}$ can to make 1 serving. How many servings can he make?

_____

Fractions: Dividing Fractions

© Steck-Vaughn Company   56   Math 6, SV 8099-5

Name _____   Date _____

•••••••••••• **"SEW" LONG FLAGS** ••••••••••••

Write the multiplication sentence.

1. $2\frac{1}{4} \div \frac{1}{8} =$ _____   **2.** $\frac{5}{6} \div 1\frac{1}{2} =$ _____

3. $2\frac{1}{3} \div 4 =$ _____   **4.** $1\frac{1}{5} \div 5\frac{2}{3} =$ _____

Find the quotient.

5. $1\frac{1}{4} \div \frac{2}{5} =$ ____   **6.** $3\frac{3}{5} \div \frac{2}{3} =$ ____   **7.** $\frac{3}{8} \div 1\frac{1}{2} =$ ____   **8.** $2\frac{1}{5} \div 1\frac{3}{4} =$ ____

9. $2\frac{2}{3} \div 6\frac{1}{2} =$ ____   **10.** $4 \div 1\frac{4}{7} =$ ____   **11.** $3\frac{1}{2} \div 1\frac{3}{5} =$ ____   **12.** $6\frac{2}{3} \div 2\frac{1}{2} =$ ____

13. $1\frac{1}{5} \div \frac{2}{15} =$ ____   **14.** $3\frac{3}{7} \div 1\frac{1}{3} =$ ____   **15.** $8 \div 4\frac{4}{5} =$ ____   **16.** $6\frac{2}{3} \div 1\frac{1}{9} =$ ____

17. $5 \div 3\frac{1}{3} =$ ____   **18.** $6\frac{1}{2} \div 2\frac{1}{6} =$ ____   **19.** $8 \div 6\frac{1}{2} =$ ____   **20.** $6\frac{1}{2} \div 1\frac{1}{2} =$ ____

21. $2\frac{1}{4} \div \frac{1}{8} =$ ____   **22.** $\frac{5}{6} \div 1\frac{1}{2} =$ ____   **23.** $2\frac{1}{3} \div 4 =$ ____   **24.** $1\frac{1}{5} \div 3\frac{1}{3} =$ ____

Real World Connection

Write the number sentence and solve.

25. A piece of material 10 feet long will be cut into pieces to make flags. Each flag will be $1\frac{1}{4}$ feet long. How many flags can be cut?

_____

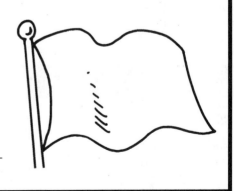

Fractions: Dividing Mixed Numbers

Name _____ Date _____

MAKING THE CONNECTION

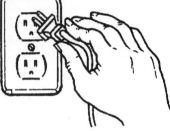

Write as a decimal.

1. $\frac{1}{4}$ = _____   2. $\frac{23}{100}$ = _____   3. $\frac{1}{5}$ = _____

4. $\frac{4}{10}$ = _____   5. $\frac{5}{8}$ = _____   6. $\frac{14}{20}$ = _____

7. $\frac{4}{5}$ = _____   8. $\frac{11}{25}$ = _____   9. $\frac{15}{50}$ = _____

Use a calculator. Find the equivalent decimal.

10. $\frac{5}{9}$ = _____   11. $\frac{1}{3}$ = _____   12. $\frac{5}{12}$ = _____   13. $\frac{1}{8}$ = _____   14. $\frac{4}{11}$ = _____

15. $\frac{5}{6}$ = _____   16. $\frac{3}{8}$ = _____   17. $\frac{7}{11}$ = _____   18. $\frac{1}{9}$ = _____   19. $\frac{1}{12}$ = _____

Write as a fraction in simplest form.

20. 0.6 = _____   21. 0.01 = _____   22. 0.20 = _____   23. 0.34 = _____   24. 0.03 = _____

25. 0.17 = _____   26. 0.09 = _____   27. 0.80 = _____   28. 0.22 = _____   29. 0.08 = _____

Real World Connection

Solve.

30. Marilyn needs to know the fractional equivalent of 0.2 in order to determine the number of servings per box of cereal. Write the fractional equivalent.

_____

Fractions: Relating Decimals and Fractions

Name _____   Date _____

····· THE "WRITE" TIME FOR PRACTICE ·····

Find the sum or difference. Write your answer in simplest form.

1. $\frac{12}{13}$
    $-\ \frac{5}{13}$

2. $\frac{1}{9}$
    $+\ \frac{5}{9}$

3. $4\frac{1}{2}$
    $+\ 3\frac{1}{3}$

4. $2\frac{1}{2}$
    $-\ 1\frac{1}{4}$

5. $3\frac{5}{8}$
    $+\ 1\frac{3}{8}$

6. $7\frac{2}{5}$
    $-\ 3\frac{1}{5}$

7. $5\frac{2}{3}$
    $+\ 3\frac{1}{4}$

8. $6\frac{1}{4}$
    $-\ 2\frac{4}{5}$

9. $6\frac{2}{6}$
    $+\ 4\frac{2}{5}$

10. $1\frac{2}{3}$
    $-\ \frac{5}{6}$

Find the product or quotient. Write your answer in simplest form.

11. $\frac{4}{5} \times \frac{3}{4} =$ _____

12. $8 \div \frac{5}{12} =$ _____

13. $12 \times 1\frac{2}{5} =$ _____

14. $\frac{1}{5} \times \frac{2}{3} =$ _____

15. $\frac{1}{4} \div \frac{1}{5} =$ _____

16. $6\frac{1}{2} \div 2\frac{1}{6} =$ _____

17. $2\frac{1}{4} \times 1\frac{1}{2} =$ _____

18. $6 \div \frac{12}{13} =$ _____

19. $\frac{1}{9} \div \frac{2}{3} =$ _____

20. $4\frac{2}{3} \times 1\frac{2}{9} =$ _____

Real World Connection

Write the number sentence and solve.

21. It took Bart $\frac{3}{4}$ hour to write one story. He wrote 8 stories. How long did he spend writing stories?

_____

Fractions: Mixed Practice

Math 6, SV 8099-5

Name _____   Date _____

Solve.

1. Andy collects baseball caps. In his collection, $\frac{1}{3}$ of his caps are blue. If he has 42 caps, how many are blue?

_____

2. Gabriel has two photo albums. One is $\frac{1}{7}$ full and the other is $\frac{4}{21}$ full. Gabriel wants to put all of the pictures in one book. Will the book be full? Explain.

_____

3. Leslie sings in a band. In one song, she claps for 60 seconds. It takes $\frac{2}{3}$ second to clap her hands. How many times will she clap?

_____

4. Becky took $\frac{1}{4}$ of her stamp collection to school, left $\frac{1}{4}$ of the collection at home, and gave the rest to her friend. What part of her collection did she give to her friend?

_____

5. Tom and Andrew are bird-watchers. One day Tom watched birds $3\frac{1}{2}$ hours in the morning and $\frac{3}{4}$ of that time in the afternoon. Andrew watched $2\frac{1}{4}$ hours in the morning and $1\frac{1}{3}$ times as long in the afternoon. Did Tom or Andrew bird-watch more total hours?

_____

Fractions: Word Problems

Name _____ Date _____

THE "WEIGH" TO MEASURE

 Complete the pattern.

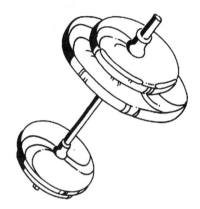

1. 0.002 L = 2 mL

0.02 L = _____ mL

0.2 L = _____ mL

2 L = _____ mL

2. 0.001 m = 1 mm

0.01 m = _____ mm

0.1 m = _____ mm

1 m = _____ mm

3. 2 kg = 2,000 g

0.2 kg = _____ g

0.02 kg = _____ g

0.002 kg = _____ g

4. 4 cm = 0.04 m

40 cm = _____ m

400 cm = _____ m

4,000 cm = _____ m

 Find the missing number.

5. 5 m = _____ km

6. 6 ml = _____ L

7. 3 mm = _____ m

8. 125 g = _____ kg

9. 0.25 m = _____ km

10. 360 cm = _____ m

11. 0.97 kL = _____ L

12. 3,000 g = _____ kg

13. 340 mm = _____ cm

14. 9 L = _____ mL

15. 2.1 m = _____ mm

16. 1 m = _____ km

17. 0.076 L = _____ mL

18. 35 cm = _____ mm

19. 14 km = _____ m

20. 3.9 kL = _____ L

21. 400 mm = _____ cm

22. 6.3 L = _____ mL

Real World Connection

Write the number sentence and solve.

23. Joey weighs 62 kg. Tony weighs 68 kg. How many grams do they weigh together?

_____

Measurement: Relating Metric Units

Name _____ Date _____

• • • • • • • • • HOW LONG? HOW FAR? • • • • • • • • •

 Choose the most reasonable estimate. Circle a, b, or c.

1. length of paper

2. length of pen

3. length of a pickup truck

a. 25 cm

b. 25 mm

c. 25 m

a. 120 cm

b. 120 mm

c. 120 m

a. 40 km

b. 4 m

c. 0.4 m

Choose the appropriate unit.

4.

diameter of a dime

5.

height of a skyscraper

6.

diameter of the earth

_____

_____

_____

 Estimate the length.

7.

8.

9.

_____ cm

_____ mm

_____ cm

Real World Connection

Write the number sentence and solve.

10. Julio drives an average of 60 km per hour on a highway. How far can he drive in $2\frac{1}{2}$ hours?

_____

Measurement: Metric Length

Math 6, SV 8099-5

Name _____ Date _____

"WEIGHT" 'TIL IT'S FULL

Change to the given unit.

1. 3 mL = _____ L   **2.** 0.24 L = _____ mL

3. 1,350 mL = _____ L   **4.** 20 kg = _____ g

5. 0.4 g = _____ kg   **6.** 310 g = _____ kg

7. 35 L = _____ mL   **8.** 5.7 L = _____ mL   **9.** 20,000 mL = _____ L

10. 33,000 g = _____ kg   **11.** 3.6 kg = _____ g   **12.** 560 g = _____ kg

13. 45,000 mL = _____ L   **14.** 6.5 g = _____ kg   **15.** 780 g = _____ kg

16. 35,050 ml = _____ L   **17.** 6.8 L = _____ mL   **18.** 26 g = _____ kg

19. 230 mL = _____ L   **20.** 47 g = _____ kg   **21.** 0.24 kg = _____ g

22. 177 kg = _____ g   **23.** 456 L = _____ mL   **24.** 1.76 L = _____ mL

Real World Connection

Write the number sentence and solve.

25. The capacity of a small glass is 120 mL. How many small glasses can be filled from a 500-mL pitcher of milk?

_____

Name _____   Date _____

Estimate the product or the quotient.

1. 35 ft × 12 = _____ in.   **2.** 3,063 ft ÷ 3 = _____ yd

3. 614 yd × 3 = _____ ft   **4.** 35,567 ft ÷ 5,280 = _____ mi

5. 75,233 in ÷ 36 = _____ yd **6.** 5,280 × 43 mi = _____ ft

Tell by what number to multiply or divide. Then change the units.

7. 36 feet to inches   **8.** 21,120 feet to miles   **9.** 66 feet to yards

_____   _____   _____

Change to the given units.

10. 346 ft = _____ yd _____ ft   **11.** 8,000 ft = _____ mi _____ ft

12. 245 ft = _____ yd _____ ft   **13.** 4 mi = _____ yd

Change to the given unit. Write the remainder in fraction form.

14. 24 in. = _____ yd   **15.** 1,760 ft = _____ mi   **16.** 86 in. = _____ ft

Real World Connection

Write the number sentence and solve.

17. Sonya buys 8 $\frac{2}{3}$ yards of fabric to make a suit. How many feet of fabric does Sonya buy?

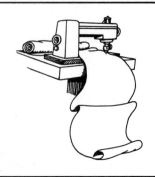

_____

Measurement: Customary Length

Name _____   Date _____

• • • • • • • • • • • • • • • TONS OF FUN • • • • • • • • • • • • • • •

 Change to the given unit.

1. 3 c = _____ fl oz

2. 2 qt = _____ pt

3. 48 oz = _____ lb

4. 8 lb = _____ oz

5. 8 lbs 3 oz = _____ oz

6. $\frac{1}{2}$ T = _____ lb

7. 2 $\frac{1}{2}$ gal = _____ qt

8. 1 $\frac{3}{4}$ lb = _____ oz

9. 16 qt = _____ gal

10. 36 pt = _____ qt

11. 12 oz = _____ lb

12. 4,000 lb = _____ T

13. 24 oz = _____ lb

14. 136 fl oz = _____ pt

15. 12 $\frac{1}{2}$ c = _____ fl oz

16. 12 $\frac{1}{2}$ pt = _____ c

17. 16 $\frac{1}{4}$ lb = _____ oz

18. 2 $\frac{1}{2}$ T = _____ lb

Real World Connection

Write the number sentence and solve.

19. Lynd's Fruit Farm sold 1,250 baskets of apples this year. Each basket weighed an average of 18 pounds. How many tons of apples were sold?

_____

Name _____   Date _____

•••••••••••• CHANGE-A-NAME ••••••••••••

Rename using the unit given.

1. 2 qt 1 pt = _____ pt

2. 3 lbs 8 oz = 2 lb _____ oz

3. 3 c 4 fl oz = 2 c _____ fl oz

Find the sum or difference.

4. 11 ft 4 in. + 2 ft 2 in.	**5.** 4 ft 4 in. + 1 ft 5 in.	**6.** 4 ft 5 in. + 3 ft 7 in.
7. 2 gal 1 qt + 2 gal 3 qt	**8.** 5 yd 3 ft + 1 yd 2 ft	**9.** 4 ft 8 in. + 5 ft 5 in.
10. 9 ft 4 in. − 4 ft 2 in.	**11.** 7 ft 3 in. − 4 ft 4 in.	**12.** 4 yd − 1 yd 2 ft
13. 7 ft 8 in. − 6 ft 9 in.	**14.** 8 ft 9 in. − 3 ft 10 in.	**15.** 6 lb 3 oz − 2 lb 8 oz

Real World Connection

Solve.

16. Alex builds a fence that is 26 yd long in 2 days.
How many feet of fence can he build in 1 day?

_____

Measurement: Using Customary Units

Math 6, SV 8099-5

Name _____   Date _____

······· GROWING TO GREAT LENGTHS ·······

Solve.

1. If Mrs. Stevens fills her watering can with 1,750 mL of
   water, how many liters is she using?

   _____

2. Garth has 342 cm of twine. If he needs 4 m of twine
   to tie up the tomato plants, how much more twine
   does he need?

   _____

3. A vine is $6\frac{1}{2}$ ft tall. How many inches tall is it?

   _____

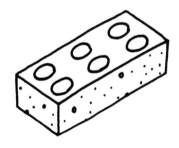

4. The entrance of the nature center is lined with 8-inch
   long bricks. One row of the bricks is one mile long.
   Are 5,280 bricks enough for one row? Explain your
   reasoning.

   _____

5. Kaye has two 750-mL bags of soil. She wants to put
   soil in a 1.5-L pot. Will the pot hold all of the soil?
   Explain your answer.

   _____

Measurement: Word Problems

Name _____   Date _____

Use Figure A for Exercises 1–2.

Figure A

1. Name three points. _____   2. Name three line segments.

_____

Tell what the symbol means.

3. $\overline{AB}$ _____   4. $\angle XYZ$ _____   5. $\overrightarrow{WX}$ _____

6. $\overleftrightarrow{MN}$ _____   7. $\overline{TU} \parallel \overline{VW}$ _____   8. $\overleftrightarrow{RS} \perp \overleftrightarrow{NP}$ _____

_____   _____

_____   _____

Use the drawing for Exercise 7–10. Tell whether
the lines are *parallel* or *skew*.

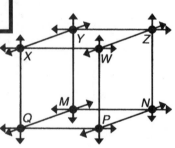

9. $\overleftrightarrow{YZ}$ and $\overleftrightarrow{MN}$ _____   10. $\overleftrightarrow{XY}$ and $\overleftrightarrow{MN}$ _____

11. $\overleftrightarrow{NP}$ and $\overleftrightarrow{XW}$ _____   12. $\overleftrightarrow{MQ}$ and $\overleftrightarrow{XY}$ _____

Real World Connection

Solve.

13. Dean draws a Four Square court with chalk. He draws
the center intersecting lines so they are perpendicular.
Does Dean draw the court correctly?

_____

Geometry: Lines

•••••••••••• **THE ANGLE COUNTS** ••••••••••••

> **Name the angles. Write *acute*, *right*, or *obtuse*.**

1. _____

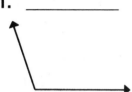

2. _____

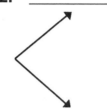

3. _____

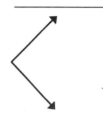

4. _____

5. _____

6. _____

> **Use a protractor to measure each pair of angles. Tell whether the angles are congruent. Write *yes* or *no*.**

7. _____

8. _____

9. _____

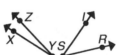

Real World Connection

Solve.

10. In art class, Rita sets a straw in a ball of clay at a 30° angle. She places another straw at a complementary angle to the first straw. What does Rita's art project look like?

Geometry: Angles

Name _____   Date _____

·········· LEARNING BY DEGREES ··········

Use the drawing for Exercises 1–6. Find and name each type of triangle.

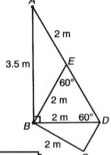

1. equilateral _____   **2.** scalene _____

3. acute _____   **4.** right _____

5. obtuse _____   **6.** isosceles _____

Write the measure of the third angle of the triangle.

7. 110°, 40°, _____   **8.** 90°, 35°, _____   **9.** 25°, 60°, _____

10. 45°, 80°, _____   **11.** 65°, 75°, _____   **12.** 15°, 90°, _____

Use the drawing for Exercises 13–16.
Write the measure of each angle.

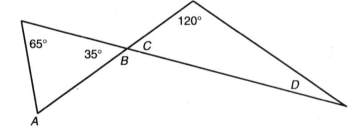

13. ∠A _____

14. ∠B _____

15. ∠C _____

16. ∠D _____

Real World Connection

Solve.

17. John is using two right triangles to build a rabbit
cage. Can his right triangles also be isosceles?
Explain your answer.

_____

_____

_____

Geometry: Triangles

Math 6, SV 8099-5

Name _____   Date _____

········ LOOKING FROM ALL SIDES ········

| Name the quadrilateral. |

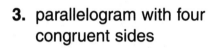

1. rectangle with four congruent sides

   _____

2. parallelogram with four right angles

   _____

3. parallelogram with four congruent sides

   _____

4. two opposite sides parallel, but not congruent

   _____

5. opposite sides parallel and congruent

   _____

6. four congruent sides and four congruent angles

   _____

| Tell whether the figure is a **regular** or an **irregular** polygon. |

7. _____   8. _____   9. _____

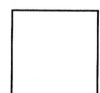

Real World Connection

Solve.

10. The teacher asks Jack to draw a rhombus on the chalk board. Jack draws a square. Did Jack draw a rhombus? Explain.

    _____

    _____

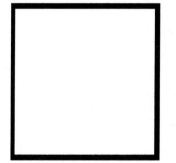

Geometry: Polygons

Math 6, SV 8099-5

Name _____ Date _____

 •••••••••• **ARE THEY THE SAME?** ••••••••••

Use the grid to draw a polygon similar to the one shown and
a polygon congruent to the one shown.

1.

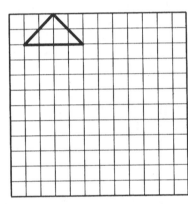

2.

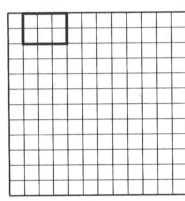

3.

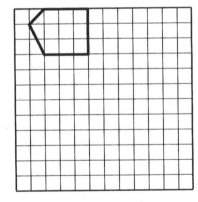

4.

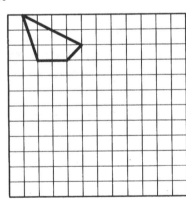

5.

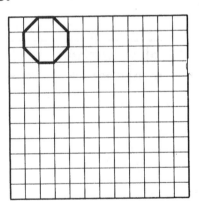

Real World Connection

Solve.

6. Marilee has 2 bowls. The bowls are similar, but not
congruent. Can Marilee store one bowl inside the
other bowl? Explain your answer.

_____

_____

Geometry: Similar and Congruent Figures

Name _____ Date _____

• • • • • • • • • • • • MAKING THE CUT • • • • • • • • • • • •

 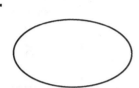 Draw the lines of symmetry.

1.  **2.** **3.** **4.**

 Complete the figures to make figures that are symmetric.

5.   **6.**   **7.**  **8.**

_____   _____   _____   _____

 Tell whether the figure has rotational symmetry. Write **yes** or **no**.

9.   **10.**   **11.**  **12.**

_____   _____   _____   _____

Real World Connection

Solve.

13. Shelbie says that she used a line of symmetry to cut a rectangular piece of cheese. Show two ways Shelbie could have cut the cheese.

Geometry: Symmetry

Math 6, SV 8099-5

Name _____   Date _____

•••••••••• ON SOLID GROUND ••••••••••

Complete the table by naming the type of solid figure.

	Type of Solid Figure	Number of Bases and Faces	Number of Edges	Number of Vertices
1.		1 base 4 other faces	8	5
2.		2 bases 8 other faces	24	16
3.		1 base	none	none
4.		2 bases 3 other faces	9	6
5.		1 base 5 other faces	10	6

6. Name three objects in your classroom that are examples of solid figures.

_____

_____

7. Name three useful common objects that are shaped like rectangular prisms. Why do you think each object is shaped like this?

_____

_____

Real World Connection

Solve.

8. Frank has four congruent triangles. What solid figure can he make?

_____

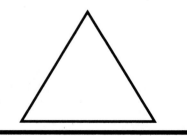

Geometry: Solid Figures

• • • • • • • • AROUND THE BLOCK • • • • • • • •

| Estimate the perimeter of the polygon. Round to the nearest whole number. |

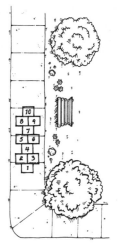

1.

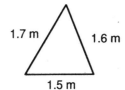

1.7 m   1.6 m

1.5 m

_____

2.

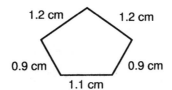

1.2 cm   1.2 cm

0.9 cm   0.9 cm

1.1 cm

_____

| Find the perimeter of the polygon. |

3.

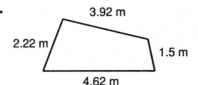

3.92 m

2.22 m   1.5 m

4.62 m

_____

4.

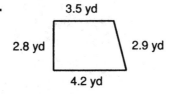

3.5 yd

2.8 yd   2.9 yd

4.2 yd

_____

5.

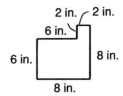

2 in.   2 in.

6 in.

6 in.   8 in.

8 in.

_____

6.

5 m

7 m   5 m

5 m

4 m

_____

7.

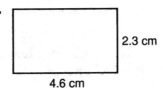

2.3 cm

4.6 cm

_____

8.

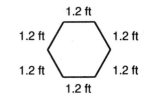

1.2 ft

1.2 ft   1.2 ft

1.2 ft   1.2 ft

1.2 ft

_____

Real World Connection

Solve.

9. Each side of the square base of the Great Pyramid Cheops in Egypt measures 115 m. What is the perimeter of the base?

_____

Geometry: Perimeter

Math 6, SV 8099-5

Name _____ Date _____

•••••••• WE HAVE YOU COVERED ••••••••

 Find the area.

1.

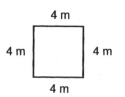
4 m
4 m   4 m
4 m

_____

2.

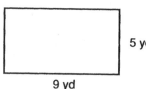
5 yd
9 yd

_____

3.
3.2 in.
4.1 in.

_____

4.

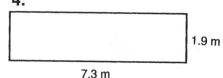
1.9 m
7.3 m

_____

5.

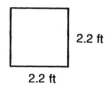
2.2 ft
2.2 ft

_____

6. $l = 7$ cm, $w = 3$ cm _____

7. $l = 11$ mm, $w = 4$ mm _____

8. $l = 5$ in., $w = 6$ in. _____

9. $l = 12$ yd, $w = 14$ yd _____

10. $l = 8$ ft, $w = 4$ ft _____

11. $l = 9$ m, $w = 0.5$ m _____

12. $l = 94$ ft, $w = 15$ ft _____

13. $l = 5.6$ cm, $w = 6.3$ cm _____

Real World Connection

Write the number sentence and solve.

14. The length of a rug is 3 yards. The width is 2 yards. What is the area of the rug?

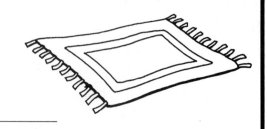

_____

Geometry: Areas of Rectangles

Name _____   Date _____

• • • • • • • • • • • • CAMPING AREAS • • • • • • • • • • • • •

 Find the area of the parallelogram.

1. $b = 4$ cm, $h = 6$ cm _____

2. $b = 14$ ft, $h = 20$ ft _____

3.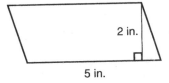

_____

4.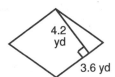

_____

5.

_____

6.

_____

7.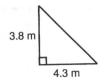

_____

8.

_____

 Find the area of the triangle.

9. $b = 12$ in., $h = 9$ in. _____

10. $b = 88$ mm, $h = 10$ mm _____

11.

_____

12.

_____

13.

_____

Real World Connection

Solve.

14. One end of a tent is a triangle. The height of the triangle is 1.5 m and the base is 2.5 m. What is the area of the triangle?

_____

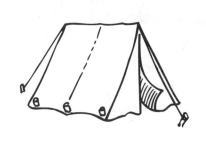

Geometry: Areas of Parallelograms and Triangles

Name _____   Date _____

········ *THIS IS HIGHLY IRREGULAR!* ·······

 Find the area of familiar shapes in Figure A.

1. Into what familiar shapes does the dashed line divide Figure A?

   _____

2. What is the area of each shape?

   _____

3. What is the area of Figure A? _____

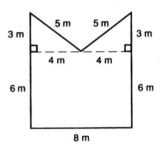

Figure A

 Look at Figure B. Find the area of the shaded part of Figure B.

4. What familiar shapes do you see in

   Figure B? _____

5. How do you find the area of Figure B?

   _____

   _____

6. What is the area of the shaded part
   of Figure B? _____

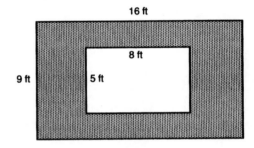

Figure B

Find the area of the shaded part of the figure.

7.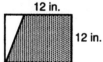

   _____

8.

   _____

Real World Connection

Solve.

9. Francine buys a rug that is 5 feet by 7 feet. She puts it in a room that is 8 feet by 9 feet. How much of the room area will not be covered?

   _____

Geometry: Areas of Irregular Figures

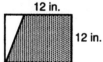

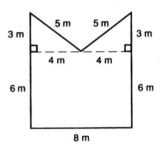

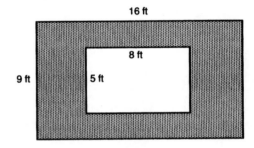

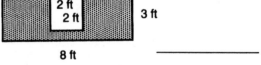

Name _____   Date _____

•••••••••••• CIRCLE AROUND ••••••••••••

Use Figure A for Exercises 1–7. Find and name the circle and its parts.

1. center _____   2. two diameters _____

3. two radii _____   4. two chords _____

5. circle _____

6. intersecting line segments _____

7. If *UV* = 5 cm, what is *VY*? *WU*?

_____

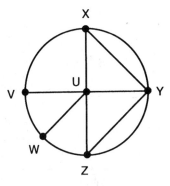

Figure A

Use Figure B for Exercises 8–12.

8. What is *AE*? _____

9. What is *BD*? _____

10. What is *AC*? _____

11. What is *CD*? _____

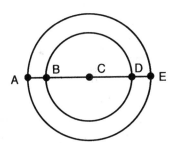

Figure B

Real World Connection

Solve.

12. A circular pond has a diameter of 100 ft. A fountain is placed in the center of the pond. How far from the edge of the pond is the center of the fountain?

_____

Geometry: Circles
Math 6, SV 8099-5

Name _____ Date _____

• • • • • • • • • • • • **MOVING AROUND** • • • • • • • • • • • •

 Find the circumference. Use $\frac{22}{7}$ for π.

1. diameter = 14 in.

2. diameter = 42 mm

_____

_____

3. radius = 14 in.

4. radius = 7 cm

_____

_____

 Find the circumference. Use 3.14 for π. Round your answer to the nearest tenth. You may want to use a calculator.

5.

3 m

_____

6.

12 m

_____

7.

18 mm

_____

8. diameter = 4 cm

9. diameter = 9 in.

10. radius = 15 m

_____

_____

_____

 Find the area of the circle. Use 3.14 for π. Round to the nearest tenth.

11. r = 10 in.

12. d = 8 in.

13. r = 5 m

14. d = 6 ft

_____

_____

_____

_____

15. r = 1.5 in.

16. d = 6.4 cm

17. r = 0.9 m

18. r = 14.4 in.

_____

_____

_____

_____

Real World Connection

Solve.

19. A furniture store delivers without charge to any location within 100 mi of the store. About what is the area of this region?

_____

Geometry: Circumferences and Areas of Circles

Name _____ Date _____

FISHING FOR VOLUME

Answer each question.

1. What dimensions do you need to know
   to find the volume of a rectangular prism? _____

2. How can you find the volume using these dimensions? _____

3. Suppose the dimensions of a rectangular prism are
   given in inches. In what units do you express the volume? _____

**Tell what numbers to multiply to find the volume of
the rectangular prism.**

4.

5.

6.
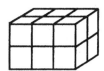

_____   _____   _____

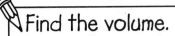
Find the volume.

7.
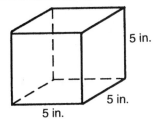
5 in.
5 in.
5 in.

8.
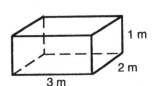
1 m
2 m
3 m

9.
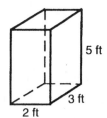
5 ft
3 ft
2 ft

_____   _____   _____

Real World Connection

Solve.

10. Dr. Chang buys this fish tank for his office.
    What is the volume of the tank?

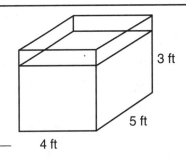
3 ft
5 ft
4 ft

_____

Geometry: Volume

Name _____   Date _____

····· PROBLEM SOLVING TAKES SHAPE ·····

Solve.

1. Geraldo took a square piece of paper and folded it along all lines of symmetry. He then drew a circle in each figure formed. How many circles did he draw?

_____

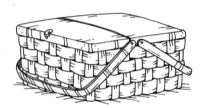

2. Maria has a picnic basket in the shape of a rectangular prism 12 in. high, 18 in. long, and 16 in. wide. She wants to cover the inside of the basket with fabric. Maria has a piece of fabric that is 50 in. by 20 in. Does she have enough fabric?

_____

3. Ines set 6 drinking glasses with circular bottoms next to each other in a row on a table. If each glass has a circumference of about 9.4 in., about what is the length of the row of glasses?

_____

4. The school parking lot is rectangular. The area of the parking lot is 2,750 m². If the length of the parking lot is 55 m, what is the width?

_____

5. A carpet costs $8.95 per square yard. What is the cost of carpeting for a room 12 feet long and 9 feet wide?

_____

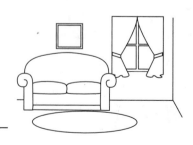

Geometry: Word Problems
Math 6, SV 8099-5

Name _____   Date _____

······· HAVING A BALL WITH GRAPHS ·······

| Use the data to make a bar graph. |

1.

| Attendance at the 1998 Football Games ||
Game	Attendance
1	78
2	85
3	62
4	109
5	99
6	75
7	124

| Use the data to make a pictograph. |

2.

| Favorite Sport ||
Sport	Votes
Baseball	35
Basketball	60
Football	45
Volleyball	50
Soccer	55
Gymnastics	30

Real World Connection

Solve.

3. Derek drew a pictograph of the number of golf clubs his dad sold each week last month. Would a bar graph show the data better than the pictograph? Explain.

_____

Graphs: Bar Graphs and Pictographs

Name _____   Date _____

Follow the instructions.

1. Use the data to make a line graph. Round the numbers to a place that is convenient.

Rainfall in Tulsa	
Month	**Rain (in inches)**
March	14.2
April	12.4
May	10.6
June	1.1
July	2.3

2. Make a double-line graph. Use a different color to display the data below on the graph you made for Exercise 1. Revise the labels on your graph.

Rainfall in Columbia	
Month	**Rain (in inches)**
March	12.3
April	10.2
May	9.5
June	4.2
July	3.1

Real World Connection

Solve.

3. Suzi is collecting data about the number of people attending the local high school's basketball games. Should she display the information on a line graph or bar graph? Explain.

_____

Graphs: Line Graphs

Name _____   Date _____

··········· MOVIE-ING AROUND ···········

Use the graph for Exercises 1-2.

1. Did Keisha spend more time on vacation or at summer school?

   _____

2. What did Keisha spend most of her time doing?

   _____

Keisha's Summer Activities

Follow the directions.

3. Make a table to show how you spent your time during a typical summer day.

Summer Day Activities	
Activity	**Number of Hours**

4. Use the table you made in Exercise 3. Make a circle graph to display the data about your summer activities.

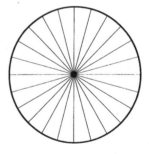

Real World Connection

Solve.

5. Sam spent $4.00 on a ticket and $8.00 on food while at the movie theater. If he went to the movies with $20.00, how much did he have left? Draw a circle graph to show how Sam spent his money. Be sure to give your graph a title.

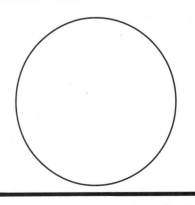

Graphs: Circle Graphs

Name _____ Date _____

········ PROBLEM-SOLVING GRAPHICS ········

Follow the instructions.

1. A newspaper reported the city's budget as follows: $10,000 for street repairs, $70,000 for building repairs, $120,00 for salaries, and $40,000 for other expenses. Draw a circle graph to show the city's budget.

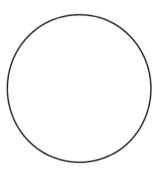

2. The high temperatures for Chicago for a 20-day period were as follows: 21°, 25°, 16°, 18°, 18°, 26°, 21°, 17°, 19°, 21°, 22°, 24°, 26°, 21°, 22°, 17°, 16°, 17°, 20°, and 25°. Make a graph to best show the data.

3. The table shows the number of revolutions per minute (RPM). If the pattern continues, what will be the RPM on speed 5? Show the data on a line graph. _____

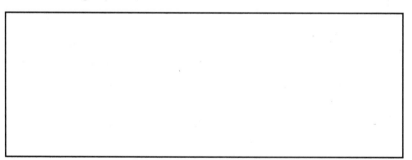

RPM of Electric Motor	
Speed 1	125 RPM
Speed 2	200 RPM
Speed 3	300 RPM
Speed 4	450 RPM

4. Use the data to make a bar graph.

Favorite Cars	
Make of Car	Votes
Ford	21
Chevrolet	15
Plymouth	24
Toyota	12
Honda	18

Graphs: Word Problems
Math 6, SV 8099-5

Name _____ Date _____

Draw a picture to show the ratio.

1. The ratio of angelfish to goldfish is 3:4.

   [ ]

   _____

2. The ratio of bass to trout is $\frac{5}{2}$.

   [ ]

   _____

3. The ratio of starfish to crabs is two to three.

   [ ]

   _____

Write the ratio in two other ways.

4. twelve to five _____

6. fifteen to twenty-one _____

8. 40:3 _____

5. 6:7 _____

7. $\frac{8}{3}$ _____

9. $\frac{7}{18}$ _____

Real World Connection

Solve.

10. There are 8 fish in 3 ponds. What is the ratio of fish to ponds?

_____

Ratios, Proportions, and Percents: Ratios

Name _____   Date _____

Write a ratio that describes each rate.

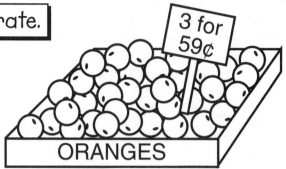

1. 3 jars for $1.99 _____

2. a dozen bagels for $2.99 _____

3. 26 mi per gal _____

4. 45 revolutions per min _____

5. 4 lb for $2.50 _____   **6.** 7 for one dollar _____

7. 55 mi per hour _____   **8.** 12 for $2 _____

Find the unit rate or unit price. Remember to express the second term.

9. 6 for $1.20 _____   **10.** $1.56 a dozen _____

11. 279 mi per 9 gal _____   **12.** 5 lb for $2.50 _____

13. 2 hours for $76 _____   **14.** 16 for $58.40 _____

15. $40 for 8 _____   **16.** $135 for 6 hours of work _____

Real World Connection

Solve.

17. Marilee buys 8 cartons of apple juice for $10. What is the unit price of each carton?

_____

Ratios, Proportions, and Percents: Rates

Name _____   Date _____

·········· PAINTING PROPORTIONS ··········

 Write the cross-products.

1. $\frac{14}{28} = \frac{1}{2}$ $14 \times 2 =$ _____

$28 \times 1 =$ _____

$28 \times 4 \not= 14 \times 2$

2. $\frac{1}{2} = \frac{8}{12}$ $2 \times 8 =$ _____

$1 \times 12 =$ _____

$1 \times 12 \not= 2 \times 8$

 Write an equation that shows that the cross-products are equal.

3. $\frac{y}{5} = \frac{4}{10}$ _____   **4.** $\frac{24}{18} = \frac{4}{n}$ _____

Write the cross-products.

5. $\frac{4}{1} = \frac{8}{2}$ **6.** $\frac{4}{5} = \frac{12}{15}$ **7.** $\frac{1}{6} = \frac{y}{18}$ **8.** $\frac{8}{x} = \frac{12}{9}$

_____   _____   _____   _____

 Tell whether the ratios make a proportion. Write **yes** or **no**.

9. $\frac{4}{7}; \frac{12}{21}$ _____   **10.** 1:6; 4:24 _____   **11.** $\frac{6}{7}; \frac{18}{28}$ _____   **12.** 9:6; 12:8 _____

Real World Connection

Solve.

13. In a painting, the ratio of tall mountains to short mountains is 5:4. In the same painting, the ratio of tall mountains to trees is 10:3. What is the ratio of short mountains to trees?

_____

Ratios, Proportions, and Percents: Proportions

Name _____   Date _____

•••••• RATIOS THAT MAKE A SPLASH! ••••••

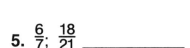 Tell whether the ratios make a proportion. Write **yes** or **no**.

1. $\frac{4}{5}$; $\frac{8}{10}$ _____

2. $\frac{8}{4}$; $\frac{2}{1}$ _____

3. $\frac{14}{24}$; $\frac{7}{8}$ _____

4. $\frac{5}{8}$; $\frac{10}{16}$ _____

5. $\frac{6}{7}$; $\frac{18}{21}$ _____

6. $\frac{3}{4}$; $\frac{7}{8}$ _____

7. $\frac{36}{42}$; $\frac{6}{7}$ _____

8. $\frac{3}{7}$; $\frac{9}{14}$ _____

 Write the cross-products. Then solve.

9. $\frac{7}{9} = \frac{n}{18}$

10. $\frac{2}{9} = \frac{m}{18}$

11. $\frac{8}{16} = \frac{r}{6}$

_____   _____   _____

12. $\frac{15}{r} = \frac{6}{4}$

13. $\frac{14}{10} = \frac{t}{15}$

14. $\frac{2}{x} = \frac{1.4}{2.1}$

_____   _____   _____

Real World Connection

Solve.

15. The ratio of adults to children at a swimming pool is 2 to 5. If there are 30 adults at the pool, how many children are there?

_____

Name _____ Date _____

PERCENTAGE POINTS

 Use the grid to shade the amount.

1. 30% 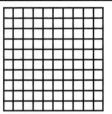   **2.** 0.5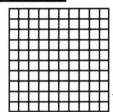

Write the decimal as a percent.

3. 0.46 _____   **4.** 0.37 _____   **5.** 0.17 _____   **6.** 0.23 _____

7. 0.2 _____   **8.** 0.8 _____   **9.** 0.07 _____   **10.** 1.33 _____

Write the percent as a decimal.

11. 19% _____   **12.** 46% _____   **13.** 2% _____   **14.** 170% _____

15. 8% _____   **16.** 89% _____   **17.** 140% _____   **18.** 4% _____

Write the fraction as a percent.

19. $\frac{3}{10}$ _____   **20.** $\frac{2}{5}$ _____   **21.** $\frac{1}{2}$ _____   **22.** $\frac{1}{10}$ _____

23. $\frac{11}{20}$ _____   **24.** $\frac{3}{25}$ _____   **25.** $\frac{3}{5}$ _____   **26.** $\frac{3}{4}$ _____

Write the percent as a fraction in simplest form.

27. 30% _____   **28.** 18% _____   **29.** 45% _____   **30.** 28% _____

31. 96% _____   **32.** 39% _____   **33.** 78% _____   **34.** 44% _____

Real World Connection

Solve.

35. A basketball player made 100 baskets. If $\frac{4}{5}$ of the baskets were 2-point shots, how many of them were 3-point shots?

_____

Ratios, Proportions, and Percents: Relating Percents, Decimals, and Fractions

Math 6, SV 8099-5

Name _____   Date _____

•••••••• PERCENTS THAT TRAVEL ••••••••

| Use a decimal to find the percent of the number. |

1. 30% of 60 _____   **2.** 50% of 40 _____

3. 80 % of 130 _____   **4.** 90% of 350 _____

5. 70% of 150 _____   **6.** 20% of 600 _____

| Use a fraction to find the percent of the number. |

7. 10% of 80 _____   **8.** 50% of 120 _____   **9.** 25% of 44 _____

10. 75% of 24 _____   **11.** 90% of 30 _____   **12.** 80% of 140 _____

| Use a calculator to find the percent of the number. |

13. 15% of 45 _____   **14.** 3% of 420 _____   **15.** 45% of 160 _____

16. 24% of 700 _____   **17.** 28% of 180 _____   **18.** 55% of 680 _____

Real World Connection

Solve.

19. Of 1,200 people surveyed, 44% preferred rail to air travel.
How many people preferred rail travel?

_____

Ratios, Proportions, and Percents: Percent of a Number

Name _____   Date _____

···· THE STORE-Y ON PROBLEM SOLVING ····

Solve.

1. Mr. Tull bought 6 videotapes and 5 CDs. What is the ratio of videotapes to CDs?

_____

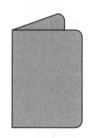

2. An office supply store sells report covers at 3 for $0.96. If the rate remains the same, how much will 10 covers cost?

_____

3. Matt bought 15 birthday invitations. He sent 40% of the cards to his friends. How many cards did he send to his friends?

_____

4. Suppose that sales tax is 8%. How much sales tax will you pay on a $15.50 shirt?

_____

5. Gerry is a member of a bookstore book club. He gets 2 books free for every 7 books he buys. If he bought 21 books last year, how many books did he get free?

_____

Ratios, Proportions, and Percents: Word Problems

SIXTH GRADE MATH
Answer Key

p. 5 1. 3,975 2. 11,745 3. 1,079,232 4. 8 r1
5. $6,341.71 6. 4 3/10 7. 36.87 8. 7 2/5 9. 5 8/9
10. $3.57 11. 6.655 12. 0.432 13. 71.4 14. 10 9/10
15. 6.874 16. 513,303 17. 9 8/9 18. 21 1/2 19. 9.93
20. 2 3/16 21. 10 1/14 22. 5 2/3 23. 1/7 24. 4/7
25. 6 1/2 26. 1.58

p. 6 1. 6 miles 2. 10 2/3 yards 3. 4 cups 4. about 6
dresses 5. 75 children 6. about 144.4 cm 7. $20.25
8. Check Students' circle graphs.

p. 7 1. 300,000; 3 hundred thousands 2. 60,000; sixty
thousands 3. 40,000,000; 40 millions 4. 474 thousand,
136 5. 12 million, 756 thousand, 827 6. 24 billion, 817
million, 526 thousand 7. 10,000,000,800 8. 96,014,048
9. 4,000,290,719 10. 10,166,020 11. 69 million, 962
thousand, 50 dollars

p. 8 1. 15.4 2. 0.003 3. 0.0018 4. 159.12 5. 2 tenths;
two tenths 6. 1.24; 1 and 24 hundredths 7. 0.0004; four
ten-thousandths 8. 22.017; 22 and 17 thousandths
9. 18 and 27 hundredths; eighteen and twenty-seven
hundredths 10. 39 and 8 hundredths seconds

p. 9 1. < 2. > 3. = 4. > 5. > 6. > 7. < 8. < 9. < 10. >
11. 4,874 > 4,784 > 4,687 12. 8.09 > 8.057 > 8.023
13. 15.820 > 15.280 > 15.000 14. 43,628 > 40,628 >
34,628 15. 395.050 > 395.009 > 395.005 16. 0.299 >
0.280 > 0.268 > 0.265

p. 10 1. 90 2. 2,700 3. $3.00 4. $9.60 5. $103.50
6. 720,000 7. 64,500-65,499 8. 25,000-34,999
9. 750,000-849,999 10. 45,500,000-46,499,999
11. 380,000 km

p. 11 1. 89,134,602,640 square inches 2. 231.73 miles
3. South Atlantic-22,432,816; Middle Atlantic-
19,315,892; North Central-18,650,621; West South
Central-8,534,534; East South Central-8,489,901; New
England-6,552,681; Pacific-4,192,304; Mountain-
2,633,517 4. 19,000,000

p. 12 1. 30 2. 103 3. 96 4. 53 5. 136 6. 28 7. 138
8. 29 9. 79 10. 55 11. 73 12. 68 13. 65 14. 48
15. 158 16. 134 17. 92 18. 71 19. 89 20. 123
21. 14 + 8 + 12 = 34 items

p. 13 1. overestimate 2. underestimate 3. 10,700
4. 2,100 5. 5,500 6. 2,200 7. 7,000 8. 2,000 9. 12,000
10. 1,000 11. 130,000 12. 70,000 13. 60,000
14. 10,000 15. 287 + 625 = about 900 stamps

p. 14 1. 1,086; 1,086 − 254 = 832 2. 439; 439 + 199 =
638 3. 9,430; 9,430 − 2,107 = 7,323 4. 15,153; 15,153
− 7,008 = 8,145 5. 3,975; 3,975 + 10,123 = 14,098
6. 16,322; 16,322 + 8,865 = 25,187 7. 430,650;
430,650 − 189,00 = 241,650 8. 5,791,266; 5,791,266 +
208,734 = 6,000,000 9. yes; 139 + 185 = 324 miles

p. 15 1. 12.5 2. 2.2 3. 0.24 4. 0.89 5. 11 6. 6 7. 39
8. 3 9. < 10. = 11. > 12. overestimate 13. underestimate
14. overestimate 15. $28.99 + $36.25 + $22.50 = about
$90.00

p. 16 1. 21.376 2. 24.843 3. 56.917 4. 351.659 5. 5.8
6. 42.62 7. $60.13 8. 72.498 9. 22.695 10. 63.469
11. 47.9694 12. 30.403 13. $86.35 14. 3,770.1 15.
10.5 + 15.85 + 8.6 = 34.95 inches

p. 17 1. 4.62 2. 11.47 3. 28.759 4. 5.85 5. 26.72
6. 89.091 7. 0.179 8. 3.649 9. 9.93 10. 13.726
11. 1.326 12. 59.02 13. 91.568 14. 17.665 15. 3.31
16. 83.035 17. 69.31 18. 560.63 19. 57.0259
20. 165.89 21. 8.36 22. 5 − (2.25 + 1.6) = 1.15 yards

p. 18 1. 388 2. 2.5 3. 483 4. $4.82 5. 113,303
6. 1,604 7. 165.89 8. 712.015 9. $20.65 10. 25,173
11. 392.01 12. 4,825.5 13. 2,130,764 14. 663.63
15. 10.026 16. 9.86 17. 1.37 18. 13.156 19. 12,713
20. 601,858 21. 181,000 − 4,192 = 176,808 cars

p. 19 1. $16.20 2. Steve's 3. 41.5 minutes
4. $5,237,767 5. $24,105

p. 20 1. b. 2. a. 3. b. 4. c. 5. a. 6. 490 7. 48,000
8. 360 9. 2,100 10. 1,800 11. 1,500 12. 400 13. 1,600
14. < 15. > 16. < 17. > 18. > 19. < 20. 219 x 38 =
about 8,000 books

p. 21 1. 5,168 2. 6,882 3. 98.571 4. 1,079,232
5. 1,613,465 6. 111,860 7. 1,785,848 8. 8,762,432
9. 5,130,600 10. 7,302,210 11. 256,208 12. 3,358,227
13. 448,812 14. 26,531,204 15. 4,278 16. 14,688
17. 4,515 18. 2,280,912 19. 264 x 25 = 6,600 oranges

p. 22 1. a. 2. c. 3. c. 4. b. 5. $48 6. 480 7. 8 8. 270
9. 100 10. 72 11. 500 12. 160 13. 14 14. 2,000
15. 4,000 16. 1.0 17. $1,000 18. 4,000 19. 8,000
20. $3.63 x 236 = $856.68

p. 23 1. 23.12 2. 11.776 3. 51.5812 4. 4.508 5. 0.7372
6. 1.8805 7. 113.685 8. 324.3 9. 3.4744 10. 18322.2
11. 23.12 12. 24.836 13. 1,596.7 14. $174.07
15. 1,925.56 16. $13.38 17. $6,341.71 18. $261.89
19. 853.2 20. $464.91 21. 310.05 22. 135.8
23. 34,368.975 24. 0.0975 25. $5.65 x 39.5 = $223.18

p. 24 1. 0.072 2. 0.0681 3. 0.4018 4. 0.990 5. 0.702
6. 947.394 7. 0.42 8. 1.7395 9. 339.69 10. 0.0588
11. 3.0105 12. 5.22 13. 1.3986 14. 0.1208 15. 118.047
16. 0.582 17. 570 18. 0.81 19. 86 20 95.6 21. 17,800
22. 4,569 23. $8.18

p. 25 1. 400 2. 15,000 3. 6 4. 1,000 5. 200
6. $1,500 7. 712 8. 50,547 9. $52.92 10. 0.014
11. 4,784.64 12. 0.0126 13. 92,859 14. 257,796
15. 736 16. $154.14 17. 2.94 18. 14,175 19. 13.806
20. 198,495 21. 15.5 x 5 = 77.5 hours

p. 26 1. 264 pictures 2. 131.25 miles 3. 2,250 miles
4. $7,770 5. 0.0288 cm thick

p. 27 a. 2. b. 3. b. 4. a. For exercises 5-21, strategies
may vary. 5. 150 or 160 6. 190 or 200 7. 600 or 420
8. 500 or 400 9. 40 10. 900 or 800 11. 20
12. 18 or 20 13. 1,300 14. 210 or 200 15. 15 16. 70
or 60 17. 160 or 200 18. 300 19. 600 20. 9 or 10
21. 70 or 80 22. 350 ÷ 12 = about 30 or 35 pans

p. 28 1. 16 2. 53 3. 3,048 4. 82 r2 5. 1,695 6. 206
7. 98 8. 3,057 9. 1,5655 r3 10. 654 11. 125 r2
12. 2,311 13. 347 r2 14. 6,369 15. 3,518 16. 4,404
17. 3,661 ÷ 7 = 523 magazines

p. 29 1. 7 r17 2. 4 3. 8 4. 8 r15 5. 48 6. 19 r97
7. 389 8. 48 r12 9. 73 10. 1,316 r26 11. 5 12. 6 r3
13. 76 14. 62 r20 15. 22 16. 17 17. 180 ÷ 27 = 6 r18;
6 bags

p. 30 1. 401 2. 320 3. 1,600 4. 2,070 r1 5. 302 r3
6. 204 r4 7. 350 r2 8. 90 r7 9. 107 10. 301 11. 604
12. 5 13. 482 14. 204 15. 5,616 16. 12 17. 480 ÷ 80 =
6 pencils

p. 31 1. 3.2 2. 1.72 3. 3.8 4. 4.2 5. 2.32 6. 0.26
7. 3.2 8. 2.46 9. 1.08 10. 0.546 11. 0.462 12. 8.52
13. 5.25 14. 0.047 15. 2.07 16. 52.7 17. 3.75 ÷ 5 =
about 0.75 pounds

p. 32 1. 12.85 2. 2.595 3. 8.425 4. 0.65 5. 7.175
6. 0.316 7. 5.95 8. 7.405 9. 3.725 10. 0.505 11. 0.365
12. 1.046 13. 0.456 14. 21 ÷ 4 = 5.25 minutes
p. 33 1. 7.3 2. 2.6 3. 37.6 4. 0.05 5. 7.6 6. 3.29
7. 43.5 8. 54 9. 4.21 10. 6.655 11. 4,510 12. 6.5
13. 34 14. 560 15. 0.64 16. 2.54 17. 3.22 18. 254
19. $232.47 ÷ $6.30 = 36.9 hours
p. 34 1. $1 2. 7 3. 3 4. 39 5. 1.1 6. $0.65 7. 2.40
8. 0.4 9. 2.858 10. 2.39 11. $7.21 12. 1.3 13. 41.83
14. 1.5 15. 32 16. $0.83 17. $2.20 ÷ 6 = $0.37
p. 35 1. 4 2. 83 r5 3. 7.2 4. 48 r4 5. 906 6. 84.7
7. 25 8. 81 9. 0.84 10. 18.5 11. 2.07 12. 206 13. 41.7
14. 68.1 ÷ 5 = 13.62 tons
p. 36 1. 85 r3 vases 2. $1.63 3. 73 boxes 4. 2 tubes;
$0.22 5. Brand A at $0.22 for each skein
p. 37 1. 8, 12, 16 2. 16, 24, 32 3. 26, 39, 52 4. 36, 54,
72 5. 38, 57, 76 6. 14, 21, 28 7. 40 8. 18 9. 28 10. 63
11. 30 12. 24 13. 48 14. 75 15. 100 16. 600 17. 12
18. 24 19. 60 20. 96 21. 240 22. 99 23. 28 apples
p. 38 1. 3/4 2. 3/10 3. 4/8 or 1/2 4. 5 5. 36 6. 30 7. 12
8. 5 9. 7 10. 4 11. 5 12. 6 13. 2 14. 2 15. 32 16. yes
17. no; 1/2, 5/7 18. no, 4/10, 1/3 19. yes 20. 18 questions
p. 39 1. 4: 12, 24; 6: 12, 24; common multiples and
denominators: 12, 24 2. 2: 4, 8; 4: 4, 8; common
multiples and denominators: 4, 8 3. 3/12, 10/12
4. 2/4, 1/4 5. 4/10, 3/10 6. 6/8, 1/8 7. 12/30, 5/30
8. 9/24, 2/24 9. 8/14, 3/14 10. 27/36, 8/36 11. 1/9, 6/9
12. 20/24, 9/24 13. 8/18, 2/18 14. 18/42, 14/42
15. LCD: 16
p. 40 1. < 2. < 3. > 4. > 5. > 6. > 7. < 8. > 9. <
10. > 11. < 12. > 13. > 14. = 15. = 16. > 17. 2/15 <
1/5 < 3/5 18. 1/8 < 2/3 < 3/4 19. 2/5 < 1/2 < 2/3
20. 3/8 < 2/3 < 5/6 21. 1/3 < 1/2 < 5/9 22. 3/12 < 2/6 <
3/4 23. Jesse
p. 41 1. prime 2. composite 3. composite 4. prime
5. 1, 2, 4, 8 6. 1, 3, 5, 15 7. 1, 2, 5, 10 8. 1, 2, 5, 10,
25, 50 9. 1, 5, 7, 35 10. 1, 2, 4, 7, 14, 28 11. 1, 2, 4, 5,
8, 10, 20, 40 12. 1, 5, 13, 65 13. 1, 7, 11, 77 For 14-16,
check students work. 14. 2 x 2 x 5 15. 3 x 5 x 5 16. 3 x 3
x 7 17. 1 by 48; 2 by 24; 3 by 16; 4 by 12; 6 by 8
p. 42 1. 1, 2 2. 1, 2, 3, 6 3. 1, 2, 3, 6 4. 1, 3, 5, 15
5. 1, 2, 5, 10 6. 1, 5 7. 2 8. 2 9. 7 10. 9 11. 5 12. 4
13. 15 14. 6 15. 6 16. 3 17. 3 18. 18 19. 18 inches
p. 43 1. 5 2. 4 3. 2 4. 2 5. 30 6. 5 7. 3 8. 8 9. 8
10. 3/5 11. 2/3 12. 2/5 13. 1/2 14. 7/9 15. 1/2 16. 9/10
17. 1/5 18. 1/3 19. 5/8 20. 1 21. 4/5 22. 4/5 23. 2/7
24. 8/15 25. 4/13 26. 5/12 27. 11/15 28. 3/5 of the class
p. 44 1. 3 2. 4 3. 7 4. 29 5. 4 6. 4 7. 5 1/8 8. 2 1/3
9. 2 7/11 10. 3 3/4 11. 9 12. 6 1/3 13. 27 14. 7 2/5
15. 64/7 16. 52/9 17. 11/4 18. 44/7 19. 27/8 20. 19/10
21. 65/8 22. 73/11 23. 3 1/3 cups of flour
p. 45 1. 1 + 1 2. 6 − 4 3. 1 + 1/2 4. 13 − 5 5. 5 + 2
6. 4 − 3 7. 1/2 8. 1 9. 1/2 10. 3 1/2 11. 1/2 12. 7 1/2
13. 1 14. 1 15. 6 16. 1 17. 10 18. 3 19. yes; estimate
by rounding-1/2 + 1 + 0 = about 1 1/2 pages
p. 46 1. 4/5 2. 2/3 3. 1/2 4. 1/6 5. 7/8 6. 1/3 7. 3/4
8. 1/7 9. 1/2 10. 1/4 11. 8/9 12. 2/5 13. 4/7 14. 7/9
15. 3/10 16. 1 17. 1/3 18. 1/2 19. 9/10 − 4/10 = 5/10
or 1/2 mile
p. 47 1. 8/12, 3/12, 11/12 2. 8/10, 5/10, 3/10 3. 5/8
4. 2/15 5. 19/30 6. 3/8 7. 9/10 8. 1/15 9. 1 7/15
10. 1/2 11. 7/8 − 3/4 = 1/8 mile shorter

p. 48 1. 7 7/12 2. 9 4/5 3. 7 7/15 4. 3 8/9 5. 16 2/21
6. 8 1/8 7. 14 4/5 8. 7 2/3 9. 5 8/13 10. 12 3/4
11. 9 5/6 12. 10 2/5 13. 16 8/9 14. 9 17/24 15. 8 3/28
16. 7 5/6 17. 17 11/15 18. 19 25/36 19. 19 61/72
20. 4 2/5 + 6 3/10 = 10 7/10 hours
p. 49 1. yes; 2 9/7 2. no 3. no 4. yes; 14/11 5. 2 5/5
6. 2 8/7 7. 5 4/4 8. 6 16/13 9. 13 3/5 10. 4 5/7 11. 3 1/5
12. 1 1/11 13. 3 10/13 14. 2 2/3 15. 1 3/5 16. 1 8/9
17. 2 1/5 18. 8 3/10 19. 5 7/8 − 3 3/8 = 2 1/2 jars
p. 50 1. 5 1/2 2. 5 5/28 3. 4 2/5 4. 5 5/12 5. 6 13/14
6. 5 1/2 7. 6 8/15 8. 5 5/21 9. 14 23/24 10. 10 2/3
11. 19 23/30 12. 11 1/15 13. 5 35/36 14. 3 13/14
15. 2 11/28 16. 4 2/15 17. 3 7/18 18. 1 3/4 pounds
p. 51 1. 1/3 2. 5/9 3. 1/20 4. 1/16 5. 2/35 6. 5/12
7. 3/40 8. 2/25 9. 5/14 10. 5/7 11. 8/35 12. 2/27
13. 1/21 14. 1/2 15. 1/8 16. 10/27 17. 6/35 18. 3/4
19. 1/3 x 1/2 = 1/6 of the students
p. 52 1. 1/1 x 1/4 2. 1/1 x 2/7 3. 1/7 x 5/2 4. 1/1 x 1/3
5. 1/5 x 2/3 6. 1/1 x 1/3 7. 1/1 x 3/5 8. 1/8 x 3/1
9. 1/2 x 1/5 10. 1/1 x 1/2 11. 1/1 x 3/5 12. 1/1 x 1/2
13. 1/2 x 1/5 14. 1/4 x 1/3 15. 1/2 16. 1/7 17. 1/6
18. 4/5 19. 1/3 20. 5/44 21. 1/12 22. 1/8 23. 1/2
24. 1/12 25. 9/16 26. 4/9 27. 1/52 28. 3/5 29. 2/5
30. 1/6 31. 5/8 x 2/3 = 5/12 of the weight
p. 53 For 1-7, answers may vary. 1. 1 2. 1/2 3. 1/2
4. 1/4 5. 20 8 6. 60 7. 480 8. 30 9. 10 10. 120
11. yes 12. yes 13. no 14. no 15. no 16. yes 17. yes
18. no 19. no 20. 52 x 3/5 = about 30 tennis rackets
p. 54 1. 7/1 x 1/5 2. 2/7 x 11/1 3. 7/3 x 8/5
4. 7/3 x 19/13 5. less than 6. between 7. between
8. greater than 9. between 10. between 11. 6 1/3
12. 5 2/3 13. 10 4/5 14. 11 7/8 15. 8 4/9 16. 4 1/2
17. 13 7/9 18. 15 2/5 19. 20 20. 3 1/3 21. 10 5/9
22. 25 23. 1 2/3 x 1/4 = 5/12 cup
p. 55 1. 3 2. 5/2 3. 1/4 4. 1/5 5. 3/2 6. 7 7. 9/2 8. 8/3
9. 8 10. 7/5 11. 5/3 12. 16 13. 3/2 14. 20 15. 3 1/3;
2/3 x 5/1 16. 4; 2/3 x 6/1 = 4 17. 5/6; 5/8 x 4/3 = 5/6
18. 3/14; 1/7 x 3/2 = 3/14 19. 1 13/15; 4/5 x 7/3 =
1 13/15 20. 3 1/3; 5/6 x 4/1 = 3 1/3 21. Ron made both
fractions in the equation reciprocal. The divisor, or the
second number, should be the only number to change.
p. 56 1. 2/3 2. 4/1; 32/1 3. 4; 5/1 4. 5/3; 5/9 5. 12 1/2
6. 12 1/2 7. 1 1/6 8. 1 3/4 9. 21 10. 16 11. 9 12. 2 2/3
13. 10 14. 2 1/10 15. 4 4/5 16. 1 1/3 17. 1 2/3
18. 2 2/5 19. 1 2/3 20. 11/24 21. 4/5 22. 8 23. 2
24. 4/5 25. 5/6 ÷ 1/8 = 6 2/3 servings
p. 57 1. 9/4 x 8/1 2. 5/6 x 2/3 3. 7/3 x 1/4 4. 6/5 x 3/17
5. 3 1/8 6. 5 2/5 7. 1/4 8. 1 9/35 9. 16/39 10. 2 6/11
11. 2 3/16 12. 2 2/3 13. 9 14. 2 4/7 15. 1 2/3 16. 6
17. 1 1/2 18. 3 19. 1 3/13 20. 4 1/3 21. 18 22. 5/9
23. 7/12 24. 9/25 25. 10 ÷ 1 1/4 = 8 flags
p. 58 1. 0.25 2. 0.23 3. 0.2 4. 0.4 5. 0.625 6. 0.7
7. 0.8 8. 0.44 9. 0.3 10. 0.56 11. 0.33 12. 0.417
13. 0.125 14. 0.36 15. 0.83 16. 0.375 17. 0.636
18. 0.1 19. 0.083 20. 3/5 21. 1/100 22. 1/5 23. 17/50
24. 3/100 25. 17/100 26. 9/100 27. 4/5 28. 11/50
29. 2/25 30. 1/5
p. 59 7/13 2. 2/3 3. 7 5/6 4. 2 1/4 5. 5 6. 4 1/5
7. 8 11/12 8. 3 9/20 9. 10 11/15 10. 5/6 11. 3/5
12. 19 1/5 13. 16 4/5 14. 2/15 15. 1 1/4 16. 3 17. 3 3/8
18. 6 1/2 19. 1/6 20. 5 19/27 21. 8 x 3/4 = 6 hours

p. 60 1. 14 caps 2. no; 1/7 + 4/21 = 1/3 3. 90 times
4. 1/2 of the collection 5. Tom bird-watched more hours.
p. 61 1. 20; 200; 2,000 2. 10; 100; 1,000 3. 200; 20; 2
4. 0.4; 4; 40 5. 0.005 6. 0.006 7. 0.003 8. 0.125
9. 0.00025 10. 3.6 11. 970 12. 3 13. 34 14. 9,000
15. 2,100 16. 0.001 17. 76 18. 350 19. 14,000 20. 3,900
21. 40 22. 6,300 23. 62 + 68 = 130 kg; 130,000 g
p. 62 1. a. 2. b. 3. b. 4. mm 5. m 6. km 7. 2 8. 30
9. 3 10. 60 x 2 1/2 = 150 km
p. 63 1. 0.003 2. 240 3. 1.35 4. 20,000 5. 0.0004
6. 0.31 7. 35,000 8. 5,700 9. 20 10. 33 11. 3,600
12. 0.56 13. 45 14. 0.0065 15. 0.78 16. 35.05
17. 6,800 18. 0.026 19. 0.23 20. 0.047 21. 240
22. 177,000 23. 456,000 24. 1,760 25. 500 ÷ 120 =
4.17; 4 glasses
p. 64 1. 400 2. 1,000 3. 1,800 4. 7 5. 2,000
6. 200,000 7. multiply by 12; 432 in 8. divide by
5,280; 4 mi 9. divide by 3; 22 yd 10. 115; 1 11. 1;
2,720 12. 81; 2 13. 7,040 14. 2/3 15. 1/3 16. 7 1/6
17. 8 2/3 x 3 = 26 ft
p. 65 1. 24 2. 4 3. 3 4. 128 5. 131 6. 1,000 7. 10
8. 28 9. 4 10. 18 11. 3/4 12. 2 13. 1 1/2 14. 8 1/2
15. 100 16. 25 17. 260 18. 5,000 19. 1,250 x 18 =
11.25 or 11 1/4 tons
p. 66 1. 5 2. 24 3. 12 4. 13 ft 6 in. 5. 5 ft 9 in. 6. 8 ft
7. 5 gal 8. 7 yd 2 ft 9. 10 ft 1 in. 10. 5 ft 2 in.
11. 2 ft 11 in. 12. 2 yd 1 ft 13. 11 in. 14. 4 ft 11 in.
15. 3 lb 11 oz 16. 39 ft
p. 67 1. 1.75 L 2. 58 cm 3. 78 in. 4. no; There are
5,280 feet in a mile. Since each brick is shorter than 1
foot, more bricks are needed. 5. yes; 750 mL = 0.75 l,
0.75 x 2 = 1.5 L
p. 68 1. X, Y, Z 2. $\overline{XY}, \overline{YZ}, \overline{XZ}$ 3. line segment
4. angle 5. ray 6. line 7. parallel line segments
8. perpendicular line segments 9. parallel 10. skew
11. skew 12. parallel 13. yes
p. 69 1. obtuse 2. acute 3. right 4. acute 5. obtuse
6. right 7. yes 8. no 9. no 10. Check students' drawings.
p. 70 1. $\triangle EBD$ 2. $\triangle AEB$ 3. $\triangle EBD$ 4. $\triangle ABD$
5. $\triangle ABE$ 6. $\triangle CBD$ 7. 30° 8. 55° 9. 95° 10. 55°
11. 40° 12. 75° 13. 80° 14. 145° 15. 35° 16. 25°
17. Yes; The sides can be congruent.
p. 71 1. square 2. rectangle 3. rhombus 4. trapezoid
5. parallelogram 6. square 7. irregular 8. regular
9. regular 10. Yes; A square has 4 congruent sides.
p. 72 1. For 1-5, check students' drawings. 6. Yes; The
bowls are the same shape.
p. 73 For 1-8, check students' drawings. 5. triangle
6. rectangle 7. hexagon 8. trapezoid 9. yes 10. no
11. no 12. yes 13. Check students' drawings.
p. 74 1. rectangular pyramid 2. octagonal prism
3. cone 4. triangular prism 5. pentagonal pyramid For
6-7, check students' answers. 8. triangular pyramid
p. 75 1. 6 m 2. 5 cm 3. 12.26 m 4. 13.4 yd 5. 32 in.
6. 26 m 7. 13.8 cm 8. 7.2 ft 9. 460 m
p. 76 1. 16 m^2 2. 45 yd^2 3. 13.12 in.^{2} 4. 13.87 m^2
5. 4.84 ft^2 6. 21 cm^2 7. 44 mm^2 8. 30 in.^{2} 9. 168 yd^2
10. 32 ft^2 11. 4.5 m^2 12. 1,410 ft^2 13. 35.28 cm^2
13. 2 x 3 = 6 yd^2

p. 77 1. 24 cm^2 2. 280 ft^2 3. 4 cm^2 4. 10 in.^{2}
5. 12 ft^2 6. 25.2 m^2 7. 15.12 yd^2 8. 7.31 cm^2
9. 54 in.^{2} 10. 440 mm^2 11. 4 cm^2 12. 8.17 m^2
13. 0.495 ft^2 14. 1.875 m^2
p. 78 1. 2 right triangles, 1 rectangle 2. 6 m^2, 6 m^2,
48 m^2 3. 60 m^2 4. 2 rectangles 5. subtract area of
small rectangle from area of large rectangle 6. 104 ft^2
7. 174 in.^{2} 8. 20 ft^2 9. 37 ft^2
p. 79 1. U 2. $\overline{VY}, \overline{XZ}$ 3. Possible answers: $\overline{VU}, \overline{WU}$
4. Possible answers: $\overline{ZY}, \overline{XY}$ 5. $\bigcirc$U 6. Possible
answer: $\overline{XZ}$ and $\overline{VY}$ 7. 10 cm, 5 cm 8. diameter of the
large circle 9. diameter of the small circle 10. radius of
the large circle 11. radius of the small circle 12. 50 ft
p. 80 1. 44 in. 2. 132 mm 3. 88 in. 4. 44 cm 5. 18.8 m
6. 75.4 m 7. 56.5 mm 8. 12.6 cm 9. 28.3 in. 10. 94.2 m
11. 314 in.^{2} 12. 50.2 in.^{2} 13. 78.5 m^2 14. 28.3 ft^2
15. 7.1 in.^{2} 16. 32.2 cm^2 17. 2.5 m^2 18. 651.1 in.^{2}
19. 31,400 mi^2
p. 81 1. length, width, height 2. multiply them
3. cubic inches or in.^{3} 4. 2 x 2 x 2 5. 3 x 2 x 3
6. 2 x 3 x 2 7. 125 in.^{3} 8. 6 m^3 9. 30 ft^3 10. 60 ft^3
p. 82 1. 8 circles 2. no 3. about 18 in. 4. 50 m
5. $107.40
p. 83 For 1-2, check students' graphs. 3. Answers will vary.
p. 84 For 1-2, check students' graphs. 3. Answers will vary.
p. 85 1. summer school 2. work For 3-5, check
students' work. 5. $8.00
p. 86 For 1-4, check students' graphs. 3. 675 RPM
p. 87 1. 3 angelfish and 4 goldfish 2. 5 bass and 2 trout
3. 2 starfish and 3 crabs 4. 12:5; 12/5 5. 6/7; six to
seven 6. 15:21; 15/21 7. 8:3; eight to three
8. 40/3; forty to three 9. 7:18; seven to eighteen 10. 8:3
p. 88 1. 1.99:3 2. 2.99:12 3. 26:1 4. 45:1 5. 2.50:4
6. $1:7 7. 55:1 8. $2:12 9. $0.20/1 10. $0.13/1
11. 31/1 12. $0.50/1 13. $38/1 14. $3.65/1 15. $5/1
16. $22.50/1 17. $1.25 per carton
p. 89 1. 28; 28; yes; 28 = 28 2. 16; 12; no; 16 ≠ 12
3. $10y = 5 \times 4$ 4. $24n = 18 \times 4$ 5. $1 \times 8 = 2 \times 4$
6. $5 \times 12 = 15 \times 4$ 7. $6y = 18 \times 1$ 8. $12x = 9 \times 8$ 9. yes
10. yes 11. no 12. yes 13. 8:3
p. 90 1. yes 2. yes. 3. no 4. yes 5. yes 6. no 7. yes
8. no 9. $9n = 18 \times 7$; $n = 14$ 10. $9m = 18 \times 2$; $m = 4$
11. $16r = 6 \times 8$; $r = 3$ 12. $6r = 4 \times 15$; $r = 10$ 13. $10t =$
15×14; $t = 21$ 14. $1.4x = 2.1 \times 2$; $x = 3$ 15. 75 children
p. 91 1. Students shade 30 squares. 2. Students shade
50 squares. 3. 46% 4. 37% 5. 17% 6. 23% 7. 20%
8. 80% 9. 7% 10. 133% 11. 0.19 12. 0.46 13. 0.02
14. 1.7 15. 0.08 16. 0.89 17. 1.4 18. 0.04 19. 30%
20. 40% 21. 50% 22. 10% 23. 55% 24. 12% 25. 60%
26. 75% 27. 3/10 28. 9/50 29. 9/20 30. 7/25 31. 24/25
32. 39/100 33. 39/50 34. 11/25 35. 20 3-point shots
p. 92 1. 18 2. 20 3. 104 4. 315 5. 105 6. 120 7. 8
8. 60 9. 11 10. 18 11. 27 12. 112 13. 6.75 14. 12.6
15. 72 16. 168 17. 50.4 18. 374 19. 528 people
p. 93 1. 6:5 2. $3.20 3. 6 cards 4. $1.24 5. 6 books